# COMPANION

# THROUGH THE

# DARKNESS

STEPHANIE ERICSSON

# COMPANION

# THROUGH THE

# DARKNESS

*Inner Dialogues on Grief*

HarperPerennial

*A Division of* HarperCollins*Publishers*

HarperCollins books may be purchased for educational, business, or sales promotional use. For information please write: Special Markets Department, HarperCollins Publishers, Inc., 10 East 53rd Street, New York, NY 10022.

FIRST EDITION

*Designed by Jessica Shatan*

Library of Congress Cataloging-in-Publication Data
Ericsson, Stephanie, 1953–
     Companion through the darkness : inner dialogues on grief / Stephanie Ericsson. — 1st ed.
     p.  cm.
     ISBN 0-06-096974-1 (pbk.)
     1. Grief. 2. Death—Psychological aspects. 3. Bereavement—Psychological aspects. 4. Ericsson, Stephanie, 1953– . I. Title.
    BF575.G7E75    1993
    155.9′37—dc20             92-53402

93 94 95 96 97 ❖/RRD 10 9 8 7 6 5 4 3 2 1

*Dedicated to*

*my Dada*

*Martha Ann Sparks*

# ACKNOWLEDGMENTS

I owe a great deal of thanks to many people—
Thank you—
To Dada, who commanded me to make books before babies.

To Rhoda Weyr, my agent, for believing in this work and selling it.

To Janet Goldstein and the people at HarperCollins for their superb work to make this book a reality.

To Bill Herbst for his initial editing, feedback and his grey chairs.

To Charlie Sugnet, my friend and teacher, who gave me *A Lover's Discourse*.

To my dear friend and sister, Negley Flinn, for the use of her Florida "dock box" when the winter rewrites in Minnesota had me frozen.

To my loyal friend Mary Farnham Whitney for the gift I will never be able to repay.

To my sweet sister, Sherry Slagle, for having to do the most painful thing of all.

To my friend in wickedness, Julia Frick Kubicek, who kept me laughing.

To Linda Hasselstrom, fellow writer and widow, who let me dump my insecurities in South Dakota so that I could do my second draft.

To Krissa Kyle, who touched me.

To Julie Ristau, who quietly championed my work.

To the *Utne Reader* for printing my first excerpt and getting the work out to the public.

To the readers of that *Utne Reader* issue who wrote me.

To Dick Obershaw and Brenda DeMott of the Burnsville Grief Center, and to the other, fellow widows who helped pull me out of the mire, and then so patiently read and critiqued the book.

To my many friends of Bill W. who stood by me without fail.

To my nanny Jennifer Barniskis, who took care of me and my daughter.

To Lenny Dee, for his cheers and support.

To Matthew Brown, my life partner and compadre, for his unconditional love.

To my daughter, who lit my life so that I could write.

And finally, to my late husband, who taught me the greatest lessons I've ever been blessed to know.

# To the Reader

This book belongs to the grieving, to the truthsayers, to the bereaved who have seen the light and the dark in one flash.

It belongs to those who have had the blinders ripped from their eyes, who suddenly see the lies of our lives and the truths of existence for what they are.

It belongs to those who feel crazy, because death has absolutely, vividly re-prioritized their lives.

It belongs to those who feel so small in the shadow of such profound truth.

It is meant to help those who are trying to fit the very sane epiphany of grief into a world that would rather have them feel insane, so as to maintain a safe status quo.

It is a book meant to ease the pain of significant loss. Its aim is not to give false comfort, but validation for the long haul. It was written to reach out in the darkness, not to altruistically give hope, for there is none, and the grieving know this unequivocally. (Ironically, however, the hope lies herein.)

Its purpose is to allow the process of redefining the self to proceed, rather than be squashed by clichés and avoidance. It is meant to defy taboos, and say what most of us dare not say, but all really think.

This book isn't written by a therapist, philosopher, theologian, or intellectual. It is written by one who—like you—has agonized, and who has humbly tried to put words to the unspeakable.

After the death of a significant person, we are suspended in limbo; we are not the persons we used to be, nor the persons we are yet to become ...

*For mourning is the constant reawakening that things are now different ...*

—*S.E.*

# CONTENTS

# CONTENTS

# CONTENTS

# COMPANION THROUGH THE DARKNESS

# THE ACT OF FATE

ABANDONMENT:

*The sudden state I am forced into.*

*I no longer belong to you.*

*I no longer belong to anyone.*

Who expects life to change suddenly? Little pocket calendars map out everyday life. *Pick up the kids. Drop off the proposal. Finish the laundry tonight. Send Mother a birthday card.* Life—listed on pages—predictable, orderly, preplanned. The priorities of daily existence are made according to our needs, and the needs of those we care about or to whom we have obligations.

Then one day, a bomb is dropped. Yesterday, there was a house—with walls, a roof, and the smells of life steaming up the windows. Today, only the rubble of disaster. Shards of broken confidence and the dust of dreams litter a cracked foundation. The calendars are forgotten. Priorities reorder themselves with "surviving" first on the list. What was eminently important yesterday is indisputably trivial today.

Like the victims of war and natural disasters, the sudden loss of someone so important plunges us into a realm where we have no control. The lives we planned will never be as we planned.

The rubble has to be swept up. But it looms like a mountain. How does one move a mountain? How do you piece together something that may someday resemble a life again? Not without many hours, days, months, even years. Not without blisters, cuts, bruises, and tears. And the only place to begin is in the shadow of the mountain.

*When you died, I was thirty-five, and two and a half months pregnant. The shock was beyond anything I could put into words, a big tumble into a blackness of sounds and cold hands clawing at me. Minutes were slow motion, and all that wasn't imperative to my survival was edited out of my memory. My psyche had been slammed against a brick wall. Every time I thought about you, about your dying alone on LaSalle Avenue in midday traffic, I felt the slam again and again. My breath was sucked out through another opening deep inside me, sucked out to oblivion.*

*Your plane was leaving in two hours. On the other end, I was driving up to meet you at the airport. So what happened? I reconstruct it over and over.*

*You took out your key and put it into the door of the car. You turned it and the door unlocked. You pulled the handle and then there was a pain. And you—what did you do? Grab your chest? Or your arm? Did you fold under the weight of it? Did you fall, hitting your head on the asphalt as cars whizzed by? When did someone see you?*

*What happened then? Did you see death? Did you say any-thing? Did you want to stay with me? Did you forget about me? Was I simply a short chapter in your life? Did you see your dead brother standing at the entrance to the white tunnel with his hands out? Did you fight death? Did you welcome it? Did you want to go? Did you think about any of us who loved you in your life? Did you know that though we were sometimes cruel, we loved you? What did you know at that moment? Did you know God? Did you even notice you'd died? Did you feel the people pounding on your chest? Were your eyes open or closed? Did you feel them pick you up and put you on the stretcher? The doctors tried for three hours to bring you back. You refused. Oh, you were as incorrigible in death as you had been in life.*

*And I? I was eating a salad in a restaurant at the hotel, after driving eight hours, pregnant and ravenous. I remember when I felt the pain through my heart. I had wanted my salad as soon as I sat down. My hunger made me watch the clock incessantly for the waiter, who had disappeared, and who didn't realize that I was about to faint. At 8:55 the salad came, and I commenced to eat, slowing myself, knowing that the hunger inside would backfire if I ate too fast. At 8:58, I felt the burn, like a hot wind blasting me open. I sat back. I tried to breathe. I couldn't. The waiter came over to see if everything was okay. I couldn't talk. I saw your face in my mind, clear and real before me. Despite the pain, I smiled, knowing I would see you coming through the airport gate tomorrow morning. Oh, two months, I thought, was too long to be away from you.*

*You were dead. You had exited the world, 2:58 P.M. Min-*

*neapolis time. In England, it was 8:58 P.M. when the vinegar curdled in my stomach. The same exact moment—thousands of miles away.*

*When you died, I was thirty-five, and two and a half months pregnant. I was alone, eating a salad in a hotel in England, going to the airport the next morning to find that my husband never got on the plane. At least, not the plane to England.*

# AFTERSHOCKS

SHOCK:

*A paralysis that starts in my soul
and quickly attacks my body.*

In Alcoholics Anonymous, there is a tradition of remembering as clearly as possible the last days or months of drunkenness. Not for maudlin reasons or self-flagellation, but because it is the lucid moment of hitting these "bottoms" that propels recovery forward. To forget is to risk the delusion that drinking again is a possibility.

So it is with death. I will try very hard to remember what the moment was like when I heard he was dead. I will try very hard to remember what the feelings were when the months afterward crawled by. These, like the last days before sobriety, are the downpayment for a new life, and new eyes. Ironically, a love of life springs from the memories of these days. Partially because I am no longer there. But mostly because I survived. Death is my friend now, my constant companion who makes me look for the precious every moment I am conscious.

And inside, I hear the words, "Be still. This won't kill you."

*First there was a rip. Like the sound of my insides being sliced by a stiletto. Time slowed to a series of still photographs. Went backward, jumped forward, into undeveloped black. Memories flashed in my head. Stupid memories. Buying a carton of o.j. with him on a Sunday morning five years ago. The look on his face when he had to do the dishes, "or else!" Nothing meaningful. But all meaningful.*

*Like a windshield hit by a rock, I shattered. Like the windshield, I was in one piece, but useless. The pieces were separate but intact, like they needed each other to exist.*

*That was all in the split second when I heard "He died." Then there was the stun. No words, no gestures. Except I found myself under the desk that held the phone that said the words.*

*People said stupid things. "Wanna cup of coffee?" I looked at them, aliens all of them.*

# THE AGONY OF GRIEF

GRIEF:

*The act of accepting forced change;*

*a constant state of my existence,*

*in varying degrees from white hot to disgruntlement;*

*a sign that I am truly alive.*

What is there to say about grief?

Grief is a tidal wave that overtakes you, smashes down upon you with unimaginable force, sweeps you up into its darkness, where you tumble and crash against unidentifiable surfaces, only to be thrown out on an unknown beach, bruised, reshaped.

Grief means not being able to read more than two sentences at a time. It is walking into rooms with intention that suddenly vanishes.

Grief is three-o'clock-in-the-morning sweats that won't stop. It is dreadful Sundays, and Mondays that are no better. It makes you look for a face in a crowd, knowing full well the face we want cannot be found in that crowd.

Grief is utter aloneness that razes the rational mind and makes room for the phantasmagoric. It makes you suddenly get up and leave in the middle of a meeting, without saying a word.

Grief makes what others think of you moot. It shears away the masks of normal life and forces brutal honesty out of your mouth before propriety can stop you. It shoves away friends, scares away so-called friends, and rewrites your address book for you.

Grief makes you laugh at people who cry over spilled milk, right to their faces. It tells the world that you are untouchable at the very moment when touch is the only contact that might reach you. It makes lepers out of upstanding citizens.

Grief discriminates against no one. It kills. Maims. And cripples. It is the ashes from which the phoenix rises, and the mettle of rebirth. It returns life to the living dead. It teaches that there is nothing absolutely true or untrue. It assures the living that we know nothing for certain. It humbles. It shrouds. It blackens. It enlightens.

Grief will make a new person out of you, if it doesn't kill you in the making.

*The denial moves in. It must be a sick joke. He's really there, and as soon as I round this next corner, he'll be there, standing with that stupid grin on his face. As soon as I open the door, he'll be there. Answer the phone, it will be him. Look in that direction, and I know, I just know I'll catch a glimpse of him. I'm sure I do see him out of the corners of my vision, but he is never there when I focus, never there when I turn my head to catch him. The man sitting at the sushi bar with the aviator glasses, like the ones he used to wear, makes me jump*

*up and then sit down quickly again, before someone sees me, looking for my husband. Not him. I speak to my friends and they all have this look on their faces like they are watching me lying on the pavement with my belly sliced open. The expression is one of mixed pity and disgust; they want to avert their eyes, but they can't. Propriety? Fascination? Did I say disgust?*

*And then there's the inertia. You know the walk has to be shoveled and instead of saying, "In a minute . . ." you say, "Maybe next week . . ." You know there are a million things to do, but you just have to sit for a while. Just for a while. And a while turns into months.*

*People say, "How are you?" and they have that look in their faces again. And I look at them like they're crazy. I think, How do you think I am? I'm not strong enough for talk. The phone rings incessantly with the damned question, how are you, how are you, how are you, how are you? Finally I say, "Fine." Just so they'll stop. And maybe they'll stop calling because they feel better now. Then one day, my strength is down, and I actually tell someone how I am and she can't handle it, she can't understand, and I never hear from her again.*

*A woman said to me, in a comforting tone of conspiracy, "My mother had breast cancer and lost her right breast . . ." "Oh," I say, "that's awful . . ." and wonder if that is supposed to be some sort of comparison . . . A tit, a husband—same thing? Strange how people try to find a common bond with your tragedy by trying to relate—they grab at the straws of a "like" experience while simultaneously they are repulsed by the agony. They see you on the street, and pretend they don't. Shit, we all have our stuff to deal with. I suppose it's hard enough dealing with your own.*

*I can't tell them to shut up, not because I'm not rude by nature but it takes so much energy to be polite . . . and I am afraid they'll go away. One more abandonment. "I lost my father two years ago . . ." and I think, Schmuck, that's supposed to happen, it's a natural part of becoming adult—children are supposed to outlive their parents. Did you have to leave your house? Did you lose the only other person in the world who would love your child the way you do? Did you lose the person you held all night, who slept next to you, warmed the bed so much you didn't need an extra blanket in the winter? Do you know how many blankets it takes to replace a husband? Did you lose the person who would worry about bills with you? Don't reduce this experience to something logical, universal. Even if it is, I walk alone amongst the dead, it's my death, my pain. Don't pretend you know it the way you know batting averages.*

*The most idiotic thing I heard was, "It was meant to be . . ." I wonder who meant it to be? Who is this grand designer who didn't consult me? And I look at them wondering if I'm supposed to feel better now. Now that they've reminded me of how totally, completely powerless I am over my own life. I invested in a person, my soul, my heart, my very body, and now I'm supposed to feel better because it was meant to be. Hah! If I ever thank God for this experience, it will be my own decision.*

*Somebody says she wants to hold me and I stand stiff and foreboding, hoping it will end soon, this too-closeness. If it doesn't end soon, if she touches me too long, I know I'll fall apart, and that could be messy. Pieces of a soul all over the pavement. Bloody shame.*

*And the conversations with God go something like this: "Oh, you imbecile, is this some kind of sick joke? Where were you* when I needed you? You're supposed to be some kind of loving God? Hah! You're fired!" And people worry about me because I'm talking to myself. Exactly, I think, I'm talking to myself because There's Nobody Out There.

The only thing I know for sure is that I don't know a bloody thing anymore. I was simply moving along, confident in tomorrows, in the next moments, in I'll-have-time-to-tell-him thoughts and some sick cosmic architect erased our future. Broadsided our lives with the crowbar of fate. I wonder if I could have seen it coming. If I really look, from now on, really watch everything carefully, maybe I'll see it coming next time and get my head out of the way of the next grand slam. Maybe I could have gotten him out of the way. I could have . . . I should have done something. And when I drive over bridges now, I'm sure they'll fall down.

The guilt emerges like a thick fog that permeates every air space available, surrounds everything, tucks itself away in corners and hovers close to the ground, waiting to trip me. What did I withhold telling him out of principle? Out of laziness? Out of a stupid confidence that I had time to tell him? Did I tell him that day that I loved him? That week? Now, the only thing I think is important was telling him I love him. I talk to the ground, to the air, to the pillow, I get on my knees on his snowy grave and weep the words into the snow, melting it, but finding only frozen ground beneath. I confess all to a dead body, waxen-faced in a coffin, that doesn't look a thing like him. I only want to crawl in next to him while I am simultaneously repulsed at the makeup morticians have smeared all over any part of him that might show.

That's grief.

# ASHAMED...

%∅ ∅%

HELPLESSNESS:

*My tendency as a wounded animal to hide,*

*or collapse into shamed passivity—*

*not because I'm to blame,*

*but because I've been overpowered.*

*I am utterly helpless.*

Exposure is the heart of shame. It broadcasts our frailties to the world, which will not necessarily treat them with kid gloves. Death exposes us, stripping us of defenses we've adapted to shield us from the blunt edges of society and life. And on some primal, almost reptilian level, we know that this exposure invites attack. Like the animal down in a pack, the taste of blood seems to override compassion. Mourning is a time when the cruelest things are said, sometimes by our most trusted. We know this instinctively when we are exposed and helpless.

Yet could it be that shame is the way we curl up and hide from the brutalities of existence? A way, once again, that our animal brains instruct us in basic survival?

*I spend most of my time curled up in the blue chair. The phone rings. I don't answer it. I cannot chance the potential pain of a bumbling condolence. You would not believe what has been said to me. The accusing eyes of other people who loved you, their off-the-cuff remarks that scrape and cut my already skinless psyche. "You killed him." Yes, someone said that. "He never loved you, you know. He loved me." That was said, too. No matter how many others said comforting things, these words kill me a little everyday as they resound against my emptiness.*

*I can do nothing about it. I am exposed. I am ashamed of my aloneness. Even though I know in my mind you didn't reject me, I feel that you did on some mysterious primal level. I feel that you dumped me. Unreasonable as this is, the feelings are ever-present.*

*So I work hard to become competent. I turn down offers for help. I don't want pity. I want you back, our old life back, our plans and dreams and hopes. I'm sliced into pieces, bleeding all over the place. Like a battered woman, I am ashamed of the gashes on my soul.*

# Awakenings

❧ ❧

COGNIZANCE:

*A momentary lapse into sanity,*

*where I realized that my insanity is a sane reaction*

*to an utterly insane event.*

To some, it will look as though we've lost our minds. We care nothing for the way we look. We are exhausted by the awakening. It is a slow lucidity emerging. Try as we might to see through the eyes of the world—the eyes the world would have us see through—we cannot speak of it to anyone. What is there to say? That we contemplate suicide, not for the theatrics of it. Not for even the end of the pain, sometimes, for even pain has become welcomed during the numb days.

And then, a small wedge of light appears under the door of our prison, and it is clear that it isn't the actual loss that makes us feel so insane, but the way others treat us.

Daily we hear the placating words of well-intentioned people. But what if they would really say what was in their thoughts? What if they would simply tell us that they would rather not see the suffering? Yet we, the bereaved, watch as others who have no idea of what we feel try to identify with us. We listen to insults that are meant as consolation, like a blind man must tolerate those who yell at him because he is blind.

Sanity is hot, searing, and far too intense to tolerate for long. What may appear to others as crazy actions are really the appropriate way to react to the sheer powerlessness that all of us face in the shadow of death.

*Go away. Don't call. And don't try to talk to me. I can't hear you. And I'm sure you won't hear me. If you want to help, bring me food. Otherwise, go away.*

# BEDS

SLEEP:

*That which eludes me.*

Sleep seems to universally elude grievers. I have never known a person in deep grief who could sleep. There is too much to think about. Every feeling that we have ever felt eddies in on us, trying to crush us in the thrust of the waves.

Sleep is not a vital function when we are faced with the meaning of existence. Our subconscious, our unconscious, our egos, our shadow selves have all been set loose together in one room to battle it out. The deep parts of us rise, as the surface parts of us submerge. It's an existential traffic jam.

We must also take good care of ourselves, for the stress of this time is so severe that our immune systems can shut down. Getting rest is as essential as it is impossible.

When the grief curdles into depression, we can also sleep too much. This is helpful. In the restlessness of it, we are processing all the changes that are taking place within.

But if sleeping or sleeplessness becomes so all-consuming that our daily obligations are neglected too long, we need to see a doctor. There is no shame in needed medication and therapy. It will help the healing process.

*The nights are interminable. I know you're there. I know you're not there. No sleep. Can't sleep. Gotta sleep. Toss, toss, toss. The bed needs changing, my sweat leaves an acrid smell in the sheets, but I can't stand to wash your smell off the pillows. The dreams come in the half-sleep, wet pillows, nightmares, black streaks from the mascara I wore the day I came home. I haven't worn mascara since. Why bother. For what? For whom? Don't care. Don't wash. Don't eat. Don't move. Gotta get some help. No one can help me. I think all the time about the times with him. About being with him now. I stand on the ledge, looking over into the inevitable canyon, and what scares me the most is that I am not afraid to jump.*

# BLACKOUTS

DISORIENTATION:
*The place I find myself in, most days,*
*which exists somewhere between the past and the present,*
*but surely isn't between freeway exits.*

Shock has rearranged our insides. The disorientation comes from not yet recognizing the new arrangement. Grief is a molting where we shed the parts of us no longer applicable to the new parts. It isn't a time to understand anything. It is a time to be a cautious driver, or not to drive at all. The world is the metaphor of our insides. The car is a metaphor for moving through our world. Since our insides are foreign to us right now, it makes sense that we are easily lost. Turning the wheel over to someone else is far safer. Soon enough, we will come to know this new world. Right now, we are strangers in a strange land without a road map.

*I woke up today on the freeway and saw a sign I vaguely recognized. I felt as if I had been away from this city for many*

*years. I felt I could find my way back home again, if only I could remember those road names.*

*I drive home. There must be an automatic pilot on my car. I get home somehow, but inside I feel panic, because I have lost control. Sometimes I don't know if I am going the right way. I don't know if the way I want to go is the right way.*

*I drive, and I talk to you. I remember you. I think about your family and I have imaginary conversations with them. In this decompression chamber of my car, I sob, I scream, I fight my way home. When I see a vaguely familiar sign, I can't seem to remember which way to go.*

*I have lost my way.*

# BLESSINGS OF
# MACABRE HUMOR

※ ❦ ※

BOOKS:

*Those things that,*
*more often than not,*
*I throw across the room.*

Few of us in the midst of a transformation can find our particular situation chronicled in books. We haunt the bookstores in search of some lucky find. The loneliness of change pushes the most inert to search for something that may indicate there have been others who have been to this place.

Yet, what we often find are words written with a distance that makes anything said lose credibility. It is usually not advice we seek. Not really, though we hope if someone can give us the magical answer, the pain might ease. On a deeper level, we seek a likeness, a way of finding comfort in the paradox in which we are suspended, a gentle stroke of encouragement that will assure us we are really in the right place, even if it all looks like such a mess. Unfortunately, few do this. Like the people in our lives, many books would prefer that we are neater about our pain. So they attempt to organize a process that is intentionally chaotic. Paradigm shifts defy order. We are well advised to keep searching, but always remember that if we are still enough, we will hear better things from within than from without.

Most importantly, it is critical that we see the confusion within as wisdom in process. The paradox is that we honestly know that we don't know anything anymore. Yet, with that realization comes a deep, lasting knowledge. It is a sane reaction to feel insulted when someone wants to explain grief to *you*, the one who knows it only too well.

*Inside of me a frenzy exists, thrusting me into bookstores, where I search for some meaning. Nothing makes any sense to me. I buy books two and three at a time, but I can read only a paragraph or two before being consumed by the dervishes in my mind. The books speak about this strange process of grieving. But I relate to nothing.*

*The writers try to explain the unexplainable to me. They try to be my teacher, when clearly I am theirs. Their words make no sense. I can see that they have been too long removed from grief, or perhaps they were never truly baptized by that fire, so that they condescend rather than transcend. I have said to one other widow—secretly, as one comrade to another—that it is tantamount to a peon trying to convince Buddha that enlightenment can be found in a bread recipe.*

*All the lies of existence have been revealed to me in the most vivid form. Logic is totally ridiculous. My mind screams at the orderly, linear pages that cheapen my transformation with labels and platitudes.*

*These literary points of view that attempt to order my chaos are supremely laughable. But my laughter is black. I fantasize about titles I could write—none of those sweet, inspirational titles for me.*

*I, too, could offend grieving people with some titles—*

*One would be a handbook. Very pragmatic. I'd call it* The Practical Guide to Surviving Armageddon.

*Then I'd do one called* Oh, Goodie, Grief! *and the sequel would be entitled* Oh, Shit, Life Again.

Dumped *would be a book I'd buy.*

*I wish that someone had written a book entitled* What to Do with Your Dead Husband's Socks. *They're always a problem.*

Bereaved No More *would be a big seller, don't you think?*

*. . . And they say I'm crazy.*

# BLOODLETTING

COUNTER-PAIN:

*Seemingly unnecessary suffering*

*which is critical to survival because it meets,*

*with equal thrust,*

*the enormity of my internal agony,*

*so that I do not implode.*

The onset of grief is a time when we stand on the ledge between life and death. It is an awakening that feels like a deadening. Relief is not found in what we normally think of as comfort. The velocity of the universal black hole sucks us into it.

In other cultures, it is not uncommon for a widow to mutilate herself after her husband's death. This would only make sense to those who have been there. She feels such torturous pain on the outside that relief seems only to be found in counter-pain. Like a migraine headache, the only thing that seems to help is to bang one's head against something harder than the pain on the inside. It is as if we know, on a cosmic level, that we will implode without some form of counter-pressure. So the self-flagellation of guilt, the remorse, the *if-only-I-had* whips, serve a very important function to the bereaved. Thoughts like, *"Oh my God, I wished him dead just a month ago!"* or *"If I had only forced him to go to the doctor . . ."* or *"This is God's way of punishing me for that affair I had twenty years ago . . ."* seem like a necessary part of healing.

None of these thoughts have any truth to them. This is not their function. It is not important that they have truth. What is important is that, in the earliest hours and months after loss, they be indulged to their fullest, for they help offset our helplessness in the face of death.

They are the essential counter-pain to internal agony.

*My body feels pain. Aches from my pregnancy. Soreness from having part of me torn off and stolen. Physical, soothing pains. There is no pleasure in them. Only relief. I feel the piercing stabs of your death. The gnawing in my chest seems to hold me together. For deeper, much deeper than I ever knew, I feel my death in yours.*

*I know it was my fault. You were alone when you died. I left you here at home while I went off to England to work. "Why can't you just write here?" I can hear you saying. Why didn't I? I don't know. I always thought you were so strong. In the past, when we'd been away from each other for days, weeks, months, it had only made things sweeter. We were a modern couple—both with careers, both with passions to pursue. I shuddered at the thought of being the "good little woman" for you. And you? You made it okay by quoting some corny coun-*

*try tune—"How can I miss you if you won't go away?" But you were only kidding. I was so selfish. What about the nights you looked at me with such sadness in your eyes?*

*And then it was I who ignored you when you refused to go to the doctor about your shoulder. I had no patience with your not taking care of yourself. And once, when we had that fight in August, I hated you so much I secretly wished you dead. Now . . . If I could take it back—I didn't really mean it!— Now, the pain inside binds me together as temporal glue.*

*Sometimes I put my dukes up, ready to take on the bastards of death. And I scream at my imaginary foes—"Come on! Go ahead, hit me!" I wish they would. It would relieve the pressure.*

# THE BLUE CHAIR

❦ ❧

INERTIA:

*The place I find myself caught in;*

*not the past, not the present, and not yet the future.*

*Utter emptiness.*

Sometimes not to move is the best move. Until now, I have had little use for putting things off. I valued being productive, and when I wasn't, I beat myself up. But now I can't move. There are good reasons to move but no motivation to back up those good reasons. As Ecclesiastes says, *To everything there is a season.* My season is today, and these months following my loss are a season of fallowness. I lie here fallow, like the earth, seemingly inert, outwardly still.

Yet inside there is something happening, like a settling of the silt after a big storm. The grains of sand have been forever rearranged. It makes no sense to do anything until all the grains have settled into their new pattern. Under the surface, the fertilizing of new life is beginning, silently, almost invisibly. I must only trust that the day will come when I plant new seeds. I cannot look to tomorrow yet, for it will use up what little of today I have. And today is so quiet. So devastatingly quiet. Yet deep down inside, I sense a payoff, if only I am patient.

Patience to me is laughable. What other alternative do I have? I cannot move. I'm shocked into a somnambulent state, and simply feeding myself seems like a major task. I am between yesterday and tomorrow. What was true about my life is no longer true. What was a day-to-day in my life is now history. What will be true tomorrow is not yet formed.

I do not choose patience. Patience chooses for me. For the first time in my life, I must be patient. There is nothing else I know how to do.

*The blue chair. The blue inertia chair. I sat there for months, waiting for you to come home. When I left that chair, I wandered through purgatory, watching others go on with their lives. I had none to go on with. You changed all that when you died. I was frozen in the moment. My sister's words, "Stephanie, Jim is dead," crackled in the sound waves just beneath my consciousness. Like a dog who hears a dog whistle, I knew there was something to be heard. Unlike the dog, I couldn't tune in. I could only sit in the blue inertia chair, frozen in the past, paralyzed about the future, avoiding as much as I could the moments that marched by in slow motion.*

*Sleep does not come. How can one sleep when one is thunderstruck? So while others sleep, while they are unavailable (unless I should appeal to their pity and call in the middle of the night), I think about the past, the future, and fill up lethargic minutes. I think about you. I think about me. I think about our baby within me. All of us inert in these moments, spending time together on your plane of existence— one-dimensional, flat and unreal.*

# BROKEN PROMISES

DEATH:

*Letting go.*

oss is life's nonnegotiable side. It is the time when we learn, unconditionally, that we are powerless over things we thought we had a grip on. But it doesn't stop there, because every ending brings a new beginning. Loss is often a blessing in disguise. I can look back on the losses of my life, the loss of my father, my family, the loss of my mother, the loss of boyfriends, a divorce, friends, the loss of years of my life to alcoholism, the loss of my ability to be a mother, the loss of my second husband, and the loss of many, many unfulfilled dreams, and I can see, in retrospect, that each one of these losses brought a blessing that would only be understood as I learned to live with the grief.

But there are times when this is a cruel message. In the penumbra of death, a widow doesn't—can't—hear: "Perhaps there is a reason behind this." In our minds, there is no good reason. God deserted us. God is cruel. Even the comforting words of friends, meant in kindness, meant to ease our grief become thorns thrust into an already bleeding wound.

Every love song, every fairy tale, every myth that promised us happy endings, lied to us. Every plan made together was a plan made with the full intention of its coming to fruition. No one told us to make contingency plans. Nor could we have carried out our dreams if we had constantly lived in fear. If we had always made escape plans, how could we have thrown conviction into our dreams?

Our world does not always make sense. And this is painfully clear to us when our dreams are crushed by forces outside our control.

I have a ninety-year-old friend who told me once that the trouble with my generation is that we expect to be happy. She said of her generation:

". . . In my day, people died. You dressed the dead. Every family lost someone—a child to the flu, a mother in childbirth, a father to TB. It was a simple fact of life. The antibiotic changed all that. Now, people don't die just as often but when they do, it is a shock to you."

There are few experiences of death to prepare us for the inevitable. As a culture, we are ill-prepared to see death as a natural experience, rich with potential for transformation and change. When we learn to reintegrate death into our growing-up experiences, we will not feel so betrayed by happily-ever-after lies.

*Once I was a fool. I stood at the edge of the cliff. I saw the chasm below. I hesitated.*

*Once I was a fool. I contemplated the cliff, not for its heights, not to soar over its depths, but to find a refuge in its darkness. I longed for the feel of plunging into it and thought only about the freedom from my pain. I never considered that it was my salvation to have a cliff from which I could jump. I couldn't realize this was opportunity, for the trickster wanted me to linger a bit, wallow in my fears, anticipate the pain and expand my reserves of fortitude. The trickster made my cliffs look appealing when my pain was too great to tolerate.*

*So there was a moment when I had had enough. I prayed to God, whom I had fired not long before (the grieving have moments of omnipotence). I asked the reinstated Master of the Universe for reprieve. And when I no longer stood alone, I jumped.*

*I didn't jump into the chasm out of courage but out of a desperate need. I had tried all avenues of avoidance available to me. Drinking was the only one I could not try, for I knew I'd never stop, never return from a bender, and that, being pregnant, would be murder.*

*No, I jumped because nothing else had worked. Once I heard that the anticipation of death was far more nightmarish than death itself. Now, I had to find out. It was not a physical death but an ego death I longed for.*

*I don't know when I jumped. There is no single moment that stands sparkling with revelations. No single time when I got the great "Ah-hah!" Perhaps it happened in my dreams. Or maybe on the freeway. When it happened is of no consequence. It happened. I jumped. I cleared the crags that would tear me into shreds. I surrendered to the wind, the gravity of the chasm's pull. I felt the utter ecstasy of death as I awakened into life.*

*I did not fall broken on the rocks at the bottom (as the wounded part of me had wished for), but rather I emerged, by the very act of falling. I laughed, for this was the ultimate paradox: falling down so that I could soar above.*

# ...By a Thread

HANGING ON:

*Something I do,*
*but I don't know why.*

Where is my safety zone? Where can I stand so that I can rest for a while as the seas of turmoil agitate around me? Is it okay for me to tuck myself away for a while, hang on to what I know, and not venture out into the storm until I am well-fortified? And when does waiting it out become running from it? I hang on. I find something buoyant, and I hold it to my breast until I am ready for the tumbling of the waves. I can allow myself a zone of safety, a time of not feeling, so I can ready myself. The time when I have to face the reality will come soon enough.

*And inside me, my baby moved, and I wondered how I would describe the funeral to her, when I couldn't remember much except the color of the podium, the blurry sea of faces looking into their laps, and the squeeze of my funeral shoes.*

# CAN'T SAY

❦ ❧

MUTE:

*The place I found myself in*
*when the reality of his death*
*collided with the daily fantasy of my life—*
*only to make all language*
*inadequate, trivial, and even untrue.*

There seems to be a natural reaction from those who wish to comfort the bereaved. Suddenly, people assume the teacher-student posture and give advice. Such an approach is incomprehensible to a grieving person. Not because we're unteachable, but because we've just experienced the ultimate reality. To assume the teaching position with the bereaved is ultimately arrogant. Grieving people have just been exposed to all the lies of our existence. The shock is a moment frozen in time that undeniably shows how ridiculous and unnatural logic is. It's like being on hallucinogens, where the boundaries vanish and perception melts. It's a time when nothing makes sense. And it makes total sense that it *shouldn't* make sense. Logic isn't remotely connected to the real nature of feeling, or thinking, or accident, or coincidence, all of which are circular and tumultuous, particularly in mourning.

The notion of the world as an orderly place is supremely laughable in grief. Wanting to help, close friends often say horrendous things like "Well, there must have been some reason it happened to you." Their motives are honorable, but they don't realize that this is sabotage to a person desperately searching for reason in an unreasonable world.

*I couldn't say much when you died. All I wanted to say was "I'm sorry." But words dwarfed the mountain of my feelings. I could have said I missed you, but that would have been like complaining about the phantom pains in an amputated leg. And it wasn't that I didn't want to complain, but rather that complaining was too small a gesture for what I needed to express. I could have said I felt guilty because I wasn't there, but what would that have mattered? I could have said I wanted to die, too, because you weren't here with me, but that would have been too revealing. Real suicides don't let on, and I wanted that option left open to me. I could have said that I was relieved, because our marriage wasn't made in heaven. We were more often catalysts for each other than companions. But how could relief exist at the same time, in the same space, as my desperate longing for you? I could have said I hated you for deserting me again. But that would have rubbed salt into my open wound. I would do this alone, in private.*

*I stand next to the casket, mute. I stand looking at a bad replica of you, something out of a wax museum. A mortician's best handiwork. I wonder why your chest is so small, but then I remember they sawed you open in the autopsy. I wonder why your nails are suddenly manicured after seven years. I stand looking at you, expecting at any moment that you will suddenly breathe, gasp for breath like you used to after you fell asleep. I expect something, and there is nothing. I wonder if you are looking at me from somewhere, either from your body or above me. But there is no sign. Not a quiver. Not a single reassurance that I ever mattered to this corpse.*

# Canonizing
# the Dead

FEAR OF BLASPHEMING:
*The reluctance I have to feel angry at you*
*because you cannot speak for yourself now.*

The fear of blaspheming holds us back from looking at the things in loss that are brutal facts. We fear our anger will injure the dead. But what would it do to the dead that hasn't already been done? Kill them? Ha, ha. Will it break the heart of the dead to know we're furious with them for leaving, still mad about their stupid, selfish habits, still fuming over the fight we had about love, or money, or sex? So what? They're dead already.

Do the dead have hearts? It may be they understand better now, anyway. Yet we fear the dead, fear that they could rise up and haunt us, that they really know now our thoughts and feelings about them. We probably have no secrets. Why else would we lock them up in caskets, vaults, six feet under the earth with a big heavy stone on top? Are we afraid they'll come back?

But how long will we allow what others might think of us (even the dead!) to control what we really feel? We do not put thoughts into our heads or feelings into our hearts. They are there. They are natural. There is a dark and a light side to all things. No one will present us with a medal if all we do is lament the good times and refuse to look at the bad times.

Even in the most perfect situations there is suffering. So it is, as well, that even in the greatest suffering there is relief.

We are, it is true, freer. If we have lost our spouse, we've also lost the parts of him that drove us nuts—the times when we could not negotiate an amicable solution to a problem, the dependence, and the prison of that dependence. This exists at the same time and in the same space as the moments of regret. Moments when, like a mother who has lost a child, we would gladly bear those problems if only we could have them back again. And this is true.

But what is also true is that there are moments when relief wafts in like a soft, autumn fog, and there is no sin in feeling it. It doesn't mean we are glad he died. It means that we are healing, that we are still alive. There are still some things, however small they are, to live for.

As Janis Joplin said in her song: "Freedom's just another word for nothin' left to lose." There is a lighter side to loss. Ironically, sometimes losing everything grants us our spiritual freedom. Like the barefoot Buddha, who needs only to beg for food and a place to sleep for the night, we have been freed of the weight of worldly possessions. The Buddha doesn't worry about making the car payment. He doesn't chew his nails over leaky roofs. He doesn't even take out the trash.

Spiritually speaking, we too, have no car, no roof, no

trash. And for the moment, in private, we can bask in this ambiguous freedom. There will be plenty of time to lament our losses.

*Strange, my urge to put you into the saint category, protect you now from criticism, from the wrath of anger. As long as I think of you as a saint, I don't have to hate you for dying. I don't have to experience the emotions I would have felt about the flaws in our relationship had you lived. It's not such an altruistic thing I'm doing when I canonize you—it's sheer selfishness. I don't want to be angry at a dead man. There is no one to scream at. It's blasphemous. You can't speak for yourself anymore. And I will never hear a plausible, comforting explanation ever again.*

*I always admired your ability to carefully, slowly consider. I admired your patience with what I would have immediately changed, not necessarily for the better, for my own comfort. But what I admired most in you—patience—was also what I most hated, because patience applied too long becomes procrastination.*

*So you made no mistakes, except for making no mistakes.*

# THE CIRCLE OF LIFE

EXISTENCE:

*I understand this state*
*only as comings and goings.*

Death brings a clarity of vision. It lets us know that there are planes of existence other than the plane we know in our limited lives. We can't measure them with logarithms, locate them on a planetary chart, weigh them with quarks and atoms, or even observe them through a scope. But we know they are there. Reason is limited to the logical, linear mind that would like to make sense of everything. The only use in this is to explain to the child-ego those mysteries that surround us.

Yet if we are to fully transform ourselves, we must allow for the possibility that more than what we know is present. We must be willing to sit with no explanation, contemplate the nonsensical, and leap with faith through the obstacles our limited minds provide to hold us back. We will feel many things, but feelings are only feelings, and thoughts are only thoughts. If we hold on to them, they will hold on to us. If we allow them to pass through us, be a filter to them, we will gain what Zen Buddhists call "the beginner's mind." It is a state of teachability and openness. Children have it oh-so-naturally.

To acknowledge that there are mysteries we will never unravel is humbling and freeing at the same time. It is not a passive stance—resigning to darkness. It is an open stance, palms to the sky, as a receiving vessel. For vessels are meant to be emptied and filled, emptied and filled, emptied and filled.

*After you died, I used to feel you only between one place and another. You died so fast that you didn't seem to know you were dead. How do I grasp your "gone-ness"? You haunt the halls of our house, the lane from our house to the road, our car—the in-between places. Never in actual places—never in rooms, never in the light. Only coming and going. Only in reflections on the windows. Only in dusks, twilights, and dawns is your spirit present.*

# COLD DRAFTS

HOLES:

*The place where he stood,*
*the incompleteness of my Self as an island*
*in a world where the individual*
*was never meant to be alone.*

. . . the first level of unity that is recognized
is that of the family. And the second level of unity,
which is deeper, is that of the tribe.
—JOSEPH CAMPBELL, *An Open Life*

There is something unnatural about being alone in a world where families, couples, and communities exist. There is shame in our isolation. We feel banished. The first days and months after loss, we limp through life with a hole instead of a shadow. The hole is there because we risked threading our lives with someone. We dared to love him and make him a part of us. Now he is gone, and there is a part of us missing. That part will never be filled again.

But the days, weeks, months, and years do begin to fill us with something new. Like the lizard who grows a new tail, we grow new spiritual parts by allowing someone else to love us the way we were once loved.

*I wonder if it is possible to be whole as a family, just me and Clio. I walk through my neighborhood in the evening with her and see the families doing the same. Can two make a family? I want to say emphatically, "Of course it can!" But what is this ache I feel in my heart, this pain in my chest when my daughter stares at a father pushing his child in a swing? Is it her ache? Is it my ache? Is it our collective ache?*

*Can I be complete and also alone? Can I make a life that is full and serene, that doesn't have the shadow of something lacking constantly following me? Will the world let me be complete? Can I, as a member of this global village, feel that I am whole if I am only one?*

*Trendy psychology says, "We cannot be dependent on others for our wholeness." I agree, in theory. I am responsible for filling my emptiness. But I do not exist in a vacuum. I am a member of the human race. The human "race"—that word is a plural.*

*I am a member of this tribe, this society. I am human. I am a woman. Yet within this tribe no place is automatically made for me, no title or identity waits for me, like a seat on a train. There are no role models. Except those in exile.*

*This is not to bemoan the tragedy one more time. I don't feel sorry for myself. I am a woman and a mother searching for safety for my child and me, a place to fit, where people don't point out our differences by treating us differently. I am looking for my place in my tribe. And I must carve out my own seat on this train. I did not ask for this job. But I do it, and tolerate the deafening silence of three o'clock in the morning.*

# The Constant Reawakening

MOURNING:

*The total insanity
that followed in the months after he died,
from which I have emerged different,
taller, stronger, more armored, more soft;
the process of sorting the seeds
into manageable, orderly piles.*

Mourning is the constant reawakening that things are now different. Put life back in order. Order? Is there such a thing as a life? Everything is changed forever. Houses have to be sold. Furniture gotten rid of. The second car traded in.

I had never used a drill in my life. Or a lawn mower. I was a whiz at sewing curtains, and great in the kitchen. Turning the switch on a drill was terrifying and exciting for me. When I hung my first hook on the wall, by myself, I felt a satisfaction I had never felt before. Never mind that it took me over a year to even go near my late husband's tools! Pride and budget made me plug that damned drill in. I was tired of men saying, "Well, it's really simple, you just do this and this . . ." And I was even more tired of paying them to do it. I was embarrassed at my dependence—me, the woman who could pull in a great salary, who could match any guy in the boardroom. Me, the woman who had traveled all over Europe on her own.

I figured if I could do those things, I could work a drill. I could fix my own car. I could make smart business investments. It only took my trusting myself.

*You started to wallpaper the kitchen. Three walls are prepped, marked, and ready. They haunt me every time I walk into the kitchen to finish them. But I've never hung paper in my life. I look at the tools in a moment of courage and shrink back intimidated. I'm sure that even if I tried, you could do it so much better.*

*The bills have to be paid, and I find that you put a few off and wonder why. I can't find the checkbook and when I do, the bank says the funds are locked up. The bill collectors call and I just cry on the phone. They start sending me notices because they can't bear my crying. The storm windows have to be put up and the snow has already fallen. The molding in the kitchen has to be painted, and all the brushes are stiff.*

*I didn't realize how many tasks you did, how many I have to do now. I walk through our house, through our life that's now merely "my" life, and the silence shouts like an angry mob at me, silently pounding inside my head, "HE'S DEAD! HE'S DEAD! HE'S DEAD!"*

# THE CONUNDRUM

MYSTERY:

*The maze of thoughts*
*I have about where you went.*

For all that there is to believe about where the dead go,
those of us who grieve know that there is no certainty
about any belief. The intellectual exercise of compre-
hending heaven, hell, and afterlife all seem alien and futile.
No one knows for certain. Only the dead. Maybe they don't
know anything at all. Maybe they're really just dead. We feel
like idiot children, awed by the finality, passive to the
answers.

First they were here next to us. Now they're gone. No for-
warding address. Not just gone for the weekend. Really
dead. They are no longer in a place named by geography. So
there are no maps to find them.

*Knowing you in this world is like lighting a candle for a*
*friend in purgatory. There is no place where we can meet, for*

*loving you in this world means loving you where there is no land to stand on, and no vessel to hold all that I have to say to you.*

*Where do I put you now? On Saturday mornings with blue-grass music orchestrating your chores? On an Irish country road with your Nikon? On the boat, heeled over on a hard beat? Where are you now?*

*We meet between Epiphany and Gethsemane.*

*I don't want you to mean anything to me. But then, who am I? And you. Did I ever mean anything to you? Me. Not your idea of me. If you're out there, listen this time. To me. Please listen.*

*Now, loving you is like being deaf in a speaking world. Like breath in the dark. Like an old man in a nursing home with a photo album. Like you-had-to-be-there situations.*

*You are my conundrum.*

# DARE I SMILE?

HAPPINESS:

*A state of being*
*that I don't believe*
*will ever come to me again.*

honestly believed that I would never be happy again. I could not have been farther from the truth. But how could I have known then what I know now? How could I have known that sheer despondency would make my moments of happiness that much sweeter? How could I have known that months of despair would lay the groundwork for years of contentment? How could I have realized that I would become so easy to please? No, there is a time when we don't believe that we will ever be happy again. And when that smile peeks out from inside, it is a surprise.

*One day, about five weeks after you died, I was happy. It was a bright and brisk winter day, and I was buying Christmas*

*presents. That day I thought about what might make my friends happy, and it made me happy. I bought funny little gifts that cost too much, and wrapped them in a rainbow tangle of ribbons.*

*I was ashamed that I was smiling. What if someone saw me happy? Would they think I was glad you had died? Was I? Don't get me wrong, I had smiled in those five weeks, I had laughed at black humor, or smiled constipated smiles that tried to relieve people of their utter helplessness. I had smiled and said I was fine to avoid the true answer. No one could do anything about my pain, and their pain, at the sight of my pain, was too much pain for me to handle.*

*This happiness was unprompted. It came from within. It came from a reinstatement of love within me. It came from getting out of myself for a few hours to give to others. It was healing. I wanted to hide my smiles, but at the same time I wanted to relish the warmth of them. I had earned these smiles. I had missed them, missed happiness. That day I began to realize that I would, someday, be happy again.*

# DEFYING DISMISSAL

🙣 🙡

EXILE:

*Banishment from my tribe,*

*my family of relatives and friends,*

*business associates and acquaintances*

*which results in heightened perspective.*

We who grieve are exiled in our society. Exiled by the turning away of a face so that they do not witness my agony. Exiled by the silence left as friends and family drift away. Exiled by the lack of recognition of this universal experience. Soon enough we sit in solitary confinement feeling as if no one else has ever felt what we feel. The irony is that what we are experiencing happens to most everyone. Why is it that our tribe dismisses us for being so pitiful in our loss when what is happening is we are growing stronger? We will eventually rise victorious, yet we are treated like cripples. The exile, the dismissal of this important time, should not be internalized. It doesn't mean that our experience is trivial, but that our society isn't ready for this caliber of enlightenment.

*How the bastards who have pitied me make me laugh. How they stumble around in their self-serving condescendence so that they might not have to jump over this cliff as I have. I chuckle at how they acknowledge little or nothing of my transformation in hopes that it won't exist. Peek-a-boo! I say to them. Go ahead! Cover your eyes, make believe death doesn't exist! Go ahead, talk down to me, make believe that I have not resided with death, dismiss my piercing eyes.*

*But I am enraged at the arrogance of their dismissal. I want to scream at them:*

*Hey, you! You are no warrior. You! You have not seen the other side! You are a pedestrian. I pity you. I can see that you are still too childlike, too small, too unready for the heat of my grief. For you—reality sits patiently waiting, like a troll under a bridge, to eat small children. Go ahead and pretend death doesn't exist, if you must.*

*Because You!—who have not lost what was everything to you, You!—who have never touched the flame, You!—who are afraid of the dark, You!—will come soon enough to the edge. Listen carefully—Your time will come. Your denial (by condescension) of my state of enlightenment/annihilation/rebirth is your way of saying you will not jump into the chasm until you must.*

*You have, however, deserted me. I stand alone in your abandonment. Alone in my singularity. Alone in the most important passage of my life. I am going on, past death. A widow friend said, "I don't take a single thing for granted now!" Her teeth were clenched the same way I find myself clenching mine in resistance. We are vigilant guardians of what is important and what is a waste of precious time.*

# DEMONS

MY SHADOW SIDE:

*Those fragments of my former life that,*

*left inside me, fester and grow,*

*challenging the new life within me.*

elf-doubts, old pain, unfaced terror—the stuff by which demons build insidious empires within us. They wait for the right time to move in—patient for the moment when a strong offensive is impossible. They are the grist of our nightmares that seep into our waking moments, undermining whatever we have come to believe in. Demons are the parts of us not yet transformed.

"We are our own demons," Roland Barthes says in *A Lover's Discourse*. Whatever mysterious forces conspire within us, we are all of them. They are not nearly as odious as we fear.

To battle a demon is to embrace it, to face it with clarity of vision and humility of the heart. To run from a demon is as effective as running from a rabid dog, for surely this only beckons the chase. Whatever we resist—persists. These demons, these parts of us that haunt us, torture us, and reduce us, are the agents of change. They throw down the gauntlet to the warrior within us to face them in a duel.

We do not change, or grow, or transform, without scraping up against our demons. They point out our shortcomings in minute detail. They know us well. Without them, we can grow soft, atrophied emotionally. They exercise our warrior spirits by forcing us to stretch spiritual tendons we rarely use. They strengthen us by resistance, as a barbell counters our muscles. As Victor Frankl once said about agony in *Man's Search for Meaning,* "If it doesn't kill us, it will make us stronger." Demons call upon the courage inside of us to do battle. Without our demons, we would grow spiritually flabby.

*I used to be fearful; now I am paranoid. I used to be a little vain; now I am totally self-centered. I used to be self-conscious; now I am ashamed to be breathing other people's air.*

*I used to be a little unsure of myself; now I am afraid the house will fall down on me. All the character defects I had before you died I now have as never before.*

*Strange—all that was is now magnified and monumental. At the same time, all that was now isn't.*

# DID I HOLD YOU DEAR ENOUGH?

CHERISH:

*The full cognizance of our love for others
that is completed only in making them
cognizant of it, too.*

here is a dangling participle, an unfinished piece of knitting, an echo that has nothing to ricochet from, when someone dies before love is fulfilled. Love sits and beckons, relentless in its pull to be consummated, yet seemingly unreachable, surrounded by the silent moat of death. How can we fulfill love alone? Is it humanly possible to be constantly aware of the divine in those around us, day in and day out? Tedium, irritation, and fatigue, are the pumice stones that chip against our moments of enlightenment to ensure that we remain human and therefore fallible.

Whether death is prolonged or sudden, few of those who are left living are prepared. So much is left unsaid. How can a son tell his dying mother that she failed him? Often, in our pity for the dying, in our guilt at being angry with them, we decide that some things are better left unsaid. But the consequences of this are far-reaching, for that which must be said and isn't will repeat itself, again and again, until, in some way, it finds its home. Sometimes, even saying *I love you* is difficult. Even if the relationship is littered with mine fields of past resentments, I know no other message we will regret not saying more than *I love you.*

Death is the great equalizer. It puts all things in their rightful perspective. It neutralizes transgressions, resentments, and disappointments. If there is only a single chance to say something,—*I love you* is the most important thing we can say to each other.

*What does it matter that you were hard? That you had your misgivings, your demands, your defenses? That you picked your nose when you drove or that you fell asleep in forty-five-dollar opera seats? I used to think you were more like a cigar-store Indian than a husband. I used to regret marrying you because you weren't what I wanted you to be when I wanted you to be it.*

*What does it matter now?*

*Did I cherish you? No, not in life. I thought you were immortal. I thought there was plenty of time to let you know I adored you. First I was going to change you. Then I would let you know I loved you. And I took it all so seriously. If I could do it all over again, I would laugh at your façade and love your cement. I would ignore your bait and bite your neck. I would cherish rather than lament that you cried three times in seven years. But what does it matter now?*

*Perhaps the most lucky thing for me was that I was preg-*

nant. I was given a life when one was taken. I lost. I gained. I was confused about it all. I found strength in the little embryo that grew within me. And weakness, too. The weakness was far more valuable. Because of the weakness, I found that I was a member of the human race. I was fragile. I was dependent. We all are frail little threads hanging on the shirt of life, one pull and we're history. One little snap and we're dead. And the only thing we really need is cherishing. Cherishing.

If I can tell anyone anything, because I know so little anymore, I would say to make sure that the people you love know it. The rest is trivial, biodegradable. It's not important, the fights, the spats, the disagreements. They are all so minuscule in the bigger picture.

What is important is that I loved you. And you knew it. When you died, maybe you thought about me, about my smiling face and the kisses I gave you for free, and all the times I laughed at your stupid jokes.

Maybe that was what you thought, right before your heart stopped.

# DISCARDING DECORUM

MANNERS:

*Limiting behavior*

*strictly meant for the benefit of others*

*to protect them from the blunt edges*

*of death, loss, and spiritual dismemberment.*

It comes like the snap of a taut wire. Our tolerance runs out. We can no longer suffer the condescending advice of people who believe they know what we're going through. We can no longer be gracious. Graciousness requires a zip of the lip, a false smile, a sensitive response—and we've run out of energy. (Isn't it strange that in the height of grief, so much is expected of us?) *Whatever you do, for God's sake, leave out the messy parts.* But we can't any longer. We need to rip off the veils.

Where is it written that we shouldn't be angry? Bitter? Rageful? These are important parts of claiming back ourselves. They require us to call upon the deepest reserves of strength within us. Unpleasant as it may be, it is freeing.

Our culture isn't comfortable with anger. There seems to be no dignity assigned to it in our etiquette. Yet anger is part of the process. Even rage. Rage at the sun for shining. Rage at the dead for dying. Rage at the living for breathing. And this rage lifts us out of the inertia, and brings back clarity.

Loss, especially sudden, unexpected loss, reprioritizes life. We see as never before the pursuits that are trivial and meaningless. The people who are really a waste of time. The institutions that pigeonhole us into roles we don't want.

So we take off the wedding band when the in-laws visit. We tell an old friend to go to hell. We sell everything, buy a motorcycle, and take a cross-country trip without a map.

We disobey.

#

*I don't know what came over me last night. We were just having coffee, two women friends and I. And something came over me. I could not listen to their words anymore.*

*"It's really time you got over this now and got on with your life." At first in my head I wondered, "What life?" Then one said, "I know what you're feeling, I just lost my father. We are all ultimately alone . . ." It sort of rolled off her tongue like a slippery oyster. I think that was the straw that cracked the back of my Miss Manners camel. I stared at her, married twenty years.*

*The other one piped up, "You think you're unique? Like no one else has felt pain?" I stared at this other alien, also married for more than twenty years. The glue that had been holding the shards of my shattered life in place melted and a monster came out of my mouth. I laughed so wickedly they looked terrified.*

*I said, "I can't believe that two women who've been mar-*

*ried for twenty years are telling me about being alone. Don't pretend you know what my grief is like! You haven't a clue. You equate losing your father to losing a husband?" To the other I said, "You think that your indulgent, existential angst about the meaning of life bears any resemblance to what I feel? Shut up, both of you. You're a couple of amateurs."*

*Any other time, I would have been horrified at my total lack of decorum. But this felt really good. I know it hurt. I know it was probably unfair. It was certainly rude. But it felt sooooo good.*

# DIVESTITURE

WILL AND TESTAMENT:

*A declaration from the grave*

*of what my values, my sentiments*

*and my loyalties have been in life;*

*an obligation I owe to the living.*

In death, we must be divested of all physical possessions before our passage can be made. Thus, the adage—you can't take it with you. Or as one friend put it—"I've never seen a U-Haul hitched to the back of a hearse."

Wills and last testaments act as a means of this divestiture—*To my son, I bequeath my business. To my wife, I bequeath our home,* and so on. In creating a will, we must imagine the time, actually emotionally visit the time when we are gone from this world. We must face that life goes on, even when ours doesn't. We must think about what we want to happen, after we are dead. Will the inheritance of money help a child? Will Mother's antique silver be safe with my brother?

The process forces us to face how we really feel about the people in our lives. And, as an exercise of such, we will see undeniably whom we trust, whom we respect, and whom we do not. If we are thinking about what might happen to our young children, we concentrate on what form of support we can enlist, even though we cannot be there. The same might be said for one's spouse. And life insurance is there to grant us peace of mind when the day comes where there is no more mind to be at peace.

For those left behind, the bequeathals are symbols of the relationship with the deceased. If a man leaves his grown children all of his estate, and his wife of forty years none, it is a powerful statement. A will is the last thing a dead person can say to the family. It may be the only time the person could be honest. Its power lies in the revelation of it after the person is silenced. There is no negotiating with the dead. There are no ways of amending relationships. There is no chance to say what has always gone unsaid. A will is a statement about the worth of the living to the dead.

Likewise, the lack of a will is also a powerful statement. One can interpret it first as the deceased's inability to face mortality. *He never thought he'd die* . . . But it can also be a profound statement to the living that the simple responsibilities owed them were not attended to. Whether there was a good reason or not, the consequences of dying intestate have destroyed families and homes.

There is no good reason, ever, for a person *not* to have a will. It is a selfish way to treat those left behind, causing indescribable havoc and additional, unnecessary pain that could easily have been avoided if the deceased had taken responsibility for their obligations. Worse, people do abominable things, not only for the money, but as a desperate

measure to assure themselves that they had meant something to the dead. It is a sad, lonely lesson in human
despair.

*I made a will today. I had to imagine being dead. I had to be
honest with what I want, and don't want. It was exhausting
and refreshing.*

# The Emptiness
# Next to Me

SILENCE:

*A loud non-noise that keeps me awake at night,*
*drives me from room to room during the day,*
*and is the sound of the wake of death.*

Emptiness has a loud sound. It is an incessant drone, like whispers we can't make out, or the sound of water draining out of the tub. I want to thrash around and get away from it. But it follows me. Everywhere, it follows me. And when there are sounds of life around me, they grate against my wounds, amplifying my own inner emptiness— the aloneness I did not choose.

There is only one thing to do. Be still. The silence will eventually become a friend. And within it, maybe we can hear what we've never heard before.

*The bed is very cold. I can't seem to sleep. I can't just lie there and wonder when I'll fall asleep. I smoke cigarettes, listen to* music, and I wait. Wait. For what? Your warm body is cold now. Our bed is cold. And I am cold. Sleep seems like an intrusion into the night, pulling me in a way I don't want to go. At the same time, I long for the descent, hoping for a dream. There are no dreams. Only feelings. Sweats, heart pounding, rude awakenings. And no memories. More amnesia.

I want you to come to me in a dream. But you're silent. No dreams. I read a little about dreams, trying to manipulate my unconscious. I think I'll try to believe in the life after, that you are out there in the cosmos and trying to call me, but you don't have the number. My old feelings of inadequacy sneak in and I think that you're probably not even thinking of me now. Only lost out there in yourself. And did I ever matter? Will I ever matter to anyone?

I feel like an intruder. How dare I want something from a dead man! How dare I keep on with this longing, long after your time is over. How dare I even fantasize into the night. Where are you out there? Come back and help me. At least for a moment. Tell me what to do. Help me in those moments. The silence is deafening. I get up and make a cup of coffee. Something to do while I wait for you never to come to bed again.

There are no comforting dreams. One of your friends told me you came to her in a dream. A friend of mine who'd never met you dreamed about you. But why won't you come to me? Why can't I have a dream, too? Why can't I see your face move and change again and not be forever stilled as a mere photograph?

It isn't fair they can dream about you and I can't. The grief experts say this is normal—that the people less invested in you will dream about you much sooner than I will. I suspect I can't afford to meet you in my dreams just yet—my spirit *knows I may not come back. May not want to stay here on this plane. And my spirit is right. "Come," I want to say, "take me with you."*

*The house makes scary sounds at night. I listen. I wait. I wait for a murderer to come and end it all. Kill me. But he never comes. He only makes noises that keep me hoping.*

# FITS OF SANITY

RAGE:

*The state I use to survive*
*seemingly endless moments*
*of intolerable pain.*

Anger is our natural protective armor. It serves us well. It tells the rest of the world that a boundary has been violated. Our society would have us swallow it, and many of us do. Those who do, die of diseases like cancer, heart attacks, strokes, and more. Anger does not simply go away if we deny it. It finds a place to reside, either in our behavior or in our bodies, or both. The longer we cap it off, and seal it from the outside world, the more it festers and grows within.

Rage is white-hot anger. It is capable of killing. It is also capable of giving life. It is a superb emotion. Used correctly, it lays down permanent boundaries, stakes out lifetime territories, and gives us girth. It will launch us out of inertia and thrust us forward. Oh, yes, rage is a useful thing.

*If it doesn't stop, I'll . . . I'll what? Drink? Die? Do what? The betrayal, the shock, the relief, the sadness, the loneliness.*

*Let me tell you about* my *death. Let me scream at you. Let me claw the frozen ground and piss on your grave for leaving me. You left. And I am left here. To continue without you. Alone.*

*Every screw I have to put into a wall, every cupboard I have to paint, every time I take the trash out to the street, I'm reminded that you are dead. You don't have to do anything anymore. You don't have to take out the trash. Or pay the bills. Or worry about my pregnancy. You've got it good. You're probably up in the cosmos, redecorating the heavens, laughing with your dead brother. Telling the same old stories.*

*But I am here. In a cold bed. Left with your messes, with your jobs, with your inadequacies. Still waiting for you to come in from the garage.*

# FORCED TO MY KNEES

❧ ❧

GRATITUDE:

*The feeling I have now for even the smallest progress,*
*for my expectations are so low I am difficult to disappoint.*

Nothing makes us grateful faster than losing someone or something that has been integral to our lives. The sudden void makes us acutely aware of everything we took for granted. The limits and boundaries of life are realigned and redefined. Kicked to a pulp by events of loss and death, we are forced to reach for help, because we realize how little we can accomplish alone. The simplest tasks, feeding ourselves, bathing, even breathing, don't only *seem* monumental—they are. Pride becomes a ridiculous defense, like a drowning man refusing a boat. Besides, being proud takes strength, something we can't remember ever having.

It seems that we are humbled before the great events of life. Events over which we have no power, no influence. Events that do not play fair. It was not these events that bring us to our knees, but our certainty that we had control. To be humbled like this is not meant to be punishment, but rather Death grooming us to awaken. In this awakening of utter powerlessness over everything outside of ourselves, something miraculous occurs. We become teachable again. Humble. Graced. In touch with powers greater than us. It feels humiliating, when ironically, it is humanizing.

*So the days roll by, like the waves on a beach. Some are big and violent, some creep up and recede without any sound at all, without my even noticing. One day blackens into another, and I tumble through them, usually unable to account for anything productive.*

*On certain days, I cannot read, or even watch the numbing programs on TV. I sit, and smoke, and look out the window until it's time to go to bed. Little by little, the days get shorter, and my energy returns. Some days I can do two or three things.*

*They said to me today that I should be grateful you died so quickly. "He didn't suffer," they said. Yet the selfish part of me wishes you had not died so fast, so I could have told you I love you. A part of me would have willingly had you suffer a little longer so I could say good-bye. I am ashamed that I could be so wicked. Their idea of gratitude is drivel.*

*Another day. Your sister, the nurse, explained your autopsy today. She said you should have been dead years ago. You were inoperably sick. Even though you ran two miles a day, ate macrobiotically, and quit smoking. You would have had to hear a doctor tell you they wouldn't want to chance surgery. They would have given you only a ten-percent chance of making it through an operation.*

*Today I am grateful you didn't know how sick you were. It would have killed you.*

# FRAGMENTS OF
# WHOLENESS

ENVY:

*When I forget that to trade places*
*with another is simply to trade problems;*
*the state I can find myself in*
*when I think that my pain, my tragedy*
*is greater than anyone else's.*

Alone, we cannot fulfill the promises broken by death. But there is a way around the disappointment, into a new paradigm of appreciation. It requires a change of agenda and brutal self-honesty. Yes, we will always be without the one we loved. Yes, our hopes and dreams will never be.

But there will be hopes and dreams that *will* be. To envy another's situation is only a way that we compare our insides to other's outsides. No matter what the circumstances, what is enviable often blinds us to the shadow and emotional cost others pay for what they have. To envy is to fail to see the grace of the only thing we really do know—our own lives. It is to underestimate the disguises of new blessings that may seem so minor compared to what we had always wished for. Yet sometime great blessings come in plain packages.

Envy is only a pedestrian way to try to feel whole when we've been fragmented. The first way to gain wholeness again is through the admission that we are not. For wholeness is not the state of total fulfillment, but a new, creative arrangement of the pieces.

The end of one story is always the beginning of another.

*When I see couples, I ache. I walk down the street, watching families of three and four, and I ache for me and my soon-to-be-born baby. Yet what is there that says that my aloneness is terrible and their togetherness is great? Neither aloneness nor togetherness promises happiness. Some of those people I envy might be miserable. Maybe they never talk. Maybe they haven't made love in weeks. Somehow, imagining this makes me feel better.*

*I have even caught a glint of envy in the eyes of some of my married friends—death is certainly cleaner than their divorces. You don't have to fight over custody of the kids. You don't have to go through the endless negotiations over silverware and stereos. Some of the older widows I know are actually relieved to be widows. They had watched their husbands retire from the company—but they still had to wash underwear, strip beds, and adhere to someone else's schedule. Now that their husbands are dead, they answer to no one—and if they want to have dinner at seven instead of five, no one pouts.*

*I want to believe that it's not a man that I need to ease my ache. If I think that my child and I will never be a real family because we are only two, I sell us short. We're enough. I really want to believe this. But there is so much to come that I am not allowed to know. And I often wonder if this isn't a time when I have to fulfill my own personal sense of wholeness.*

# GHOST DREAD

INTUITIONS:

*The awareness I have*
*that there are other planes of existence*
*operating outside of my realm of understanding.*

Intuition is another form of intelligence. It is an awareness of something other than ourselves that influences us. It is a sense of the mysteries of life that defy explanation. We rarely acknowledge intuition in our left-brain culture, most probably because we can't measure it, or locate it in our bodies. We worship the brain, logical, linear, book-smart intelligence, and prefer to believe that it is the only form. So it is relegated to tabloid descriptions like ESP and dismissed.

Yet few animals are without it. Why does a dog growl at some people and not others? Why do children shy away from some people and go open-armed to others? How did Einstein discover the theory of relativity? How do the squirrels know to grow thicker coats when there is a hard winter coming? How do animals know when an earthquake is coming? How do we sometimes know who is calling us before we answer the phone? How does a mother hear her child two blocks away?

It is our intuition. It is the ears and eyes we have inside, observing always what we cannot see. It is a voice or an image that is integrally woven into a larger, collective information bank. It comes to us when we still our thoughts. It will shout through the noise to us when we are extraordinarily vulnerable. As we begin to let go of the one who died, our intuition will let us feel them so that we can say our good-byes.

*When I get up in the middle of the night and go to the kitchen for a glass of water, I think I'm going to bump into you. The late you. I feel you walking around our house, but only in the halls, and only when there are no lights on. You now seem to exist only between places, coming and going. But the hole you left behind exists in every room, every chamber of my heart, every corner where we walked together. The hole is like a mirror into another mirror, giving endless form to the holes left in my life. I relive them all, simultaneously, and I have to go to bed for a day.*

# GOD WHO?

ALONE:

*The belief that there is no higher order,*

*only random acts of cruelty*

*or coincidental acts of kindness.*

*It is hell.*

To be fully alive is to be in a constant state of grief. We will lose many things, people, dreams. It is the state of existence called maturity. Some of us will lose merely a few dreams, maybe one parent, perhaps both. All of us will suffer the loss of our teenage omnipotence; our illusions about grown-up-hood as the cure for the aches of youth; our fantasies about living "happily ever after" in love; our youthful firmness to the softness of maturing bodies. Some of us will lose more: our homes, our professions, our sense of worth in society. Then there are the "Jobs" who will lose the hardest things to let go of: spouses, children, best friends, cultures, even homelands. And like Job, we will beat our chests before God and ask over and over, "Why, God? What have I done to deserve this? Why hast thou forsaken me?"

*I fired God that day. I hated God that day. I still hate God. But now I'm forced to believe in some kind of god, simply because if I am to continue living, the silence of the Great Alone is too much. Perhaps someday I'll feel like asking God for forgiveness for these words, but now I am only rageful that I have no choices but total desolation in atheism, or to believe in such a cruel fool as Him.*

*Once in a while, a faint shadow of hope appears at my heels. Is there synchronicity in these events that will lead to a greater gift than I can now imagine? Can there be a reason that fits into a design, in which I am simply a movable pawn? Should anyone tell me today there was a reason that it all happened, I would try to rip off their lips. I would feel insulted. Yet why don't I feel insulted when that small voice inside of me nudges me along with barely audible whispers of hope? Perhaps I am simply too proud to think that someone else could see my life clearer than I can. Yet, privately, I'm sure it's true. You used to smile at me.*

*Someday, I'll surprise myself. Someday, I'll rejoin the ranks of the living, and not think about you every moment of every day. One day, I want to speak the unspeakable—the things I could not say, not for their secrecy, but for their honesty. Inside, I hear a voice that tells me I will understand how your dying fit into a greater scheme of things. But even four months later, I still stubbornly think God is a bumbling idiot.*

# GONE

DEAD:

*The act of goneness,*
*an incomprehensible event*
*that leaves me mute.*

We cannot walk out of the darkness unless we are first willing to immerse ourselves fully in it. It demands a leap of faith, for there are no signposts along the way that will guarantee our safe return. There is only a dark tunnel, leading to who-knows-where. We know the danger, we feel it in our adrenaline, pumping blood through our bodies at frightening speed. We know, intuitively, that we may never come out of the blackness. But there is no choice, for to be fully alive we must die with our losses. This is a moment in time when we succumb to death, so that we may live.

*I wander through the house*
*In the middle of the night,*
*Feeling you in the halls,*

*Anticipating that I will bump into you.*
*Hoping, fearing, that I will feel your body*
*One last time.*
*I look out the windows at night,*
*The reflection of the lights inside*
*Shoot back the image of the room.*
*And in the translucence*
*Of those images,*
*I wait for your face to appear,*
*Out of the ethers,*
*Out of the night,*
*Out of death.*

*Saturday night, I got it.*
*You're gone.*
*I never did get "Dead,"*
*But that night, I got "Gone."*
*Gone so that I will never see you*
*Walking toward me*
*Down a crowded street.*
*Gone so that I won't ever hear you*
*Pounding nails*
*In the basement.*
*Gone so that when I set the table*
*For two accidentally,*
*You won't show up.*

*Yesterday, I opened the door to call the dog,*
*And instead of his name, I called yours.*

# THE "GOOD WIDOW" RUBBISH

COMPADRE:

*Like a fellow POW,*

*the only other person who can sit across from me,*

*and I know they know what I know.*

The honesty of the deeply bereaved is refreshing. In the shock of loss, we grow finely tuned antennae for bullshit. We are gifted with unbridled, uncensored honesty.

I have heard laughter from a group of widows like no other laughter. The freedom we found by looking into already-knowing eyes set us loose. What I thought would be a bunch of old ladies pounding their breasts and lamenting dead husbands turned out to be an uproarious cache of women my own age and even younger who turned their feelings about truly gruesome events into searing black humor. What we spoke would have shocked and offended the general public. But the honesty granted us freedom.

As members of an elite club (which, by the way, no one wants to join) we healed each other with our dark wit, our scathing stories, and our newborn strength. We had already paid the dues of membership by losing what we most valued, and so we had no fear about saying what was really on our minds.

We rolled our eyes in conspiracy at the clumsy things people say to grieving widows. We raged at the dead. We cried, and kept talking through our tears. We stood up tall and unashamed when we realized that we *weren't* devastated, that we didn't have to die with the dead. We rebelled against convention and wore red. We giggled like schoolgirls when we talked about our first postmortem sexual experiences.

We healed each other by speaking the unspeakable. In the safety of one another's company, where we would offend no one, and hurt neither ourselves nor others, we *grieved*—something not allowed in the world at large.

Stripped of all dignity, we had little use for façades. Robbed of our natural social defenses and manners, we basked in knowing exactly what each of us was feeling. Death had taught us to be alone, but our togetherness in being alone sweetened the irony.

*I met her at a restaurant—another widow, a fellow traveler on the long road of grief. After a brief introduction, we fell together like two women who had been reared from the same womb. Never an awkward or self-conscious moment passed between us, only the magnetism of two Psyches who had been to the edge of*

*the pool, had considered throwing themselves in, but had instead turned away from the abyss (at Pan's [pan-icked?] urging) to sort the seeds of Aphrodite.*

*Sort, sort, sort, the worker-ant parts of us had sifted through papers, through inner dialogues, through outer conventions that would have us silenced, even through our dead men's clothing in search of the smell of them.*

*Sort, sort, sort, through the ex-wives and the damaged children, the deeds to land, the monumental probate attorney fees. Through the language of laws that would leave us feeling like idiots, through the language of cultural taboos that would have us tell the world that we are "just fine" when our ribs ache for the feel of our men against us, through the language of grief books that say all the same things but desert us by leaving the unsafe things unsaid.*

*We sat and sorted. First she spoke, then I spoke. We looked at each other and knew. We cried tears—not for the other (for grief is selfish and self-centered), but for the relief of not being the only person in this world to feel what we felt. In the space between us that was littered with napkins, forks, half-eaten plates of food, we touched. Not a hand, not a hug, but simply spirits touching. Overlapping, hungry, lonely, starving spirits, realizing how devastating the longing had been by the momentary relief from it.*

*Another writer-widow, or is that widow-writer? You sat, composed around the edges, unremarkable no doubt to those at the next table. With your denim skirt and jacket, a Black Hills Rancher Woman-Widow-Writer. No one could have known that tongues were being spoken. Perhaps the waiter knew, for he dutifully approached us often, only to back off immediately, sacrificing his good service to the intense momentum of our privacy.*

*Often I looked up while speaking to see tears glistening from behind your wire rims. I knew you knew that I knew what you knew. We are a minuscule, elite club of people who have unwittingly, unwillingly, and somehow blessedly traveled through the gardens of Gethsemane, fated to know what all of us in this world would rather not face, privy to the face of death and life, a two-faced mask. Our loneliness? Though it is our hair shirt, we would no sooner have it taken from us than we would have our eyes punctured out of our heads. There is an Ecstatic Angst bestowed (at any given moment) on a privileged few, those of us who thank no one for this cross that seems to be our destruction and resurrection in one. This terrible beauty. We lose the one closest to us to gain the one inside.*

*You spoke with an authenticity that made your simple explanations reverberate with enormous truths, truths that seemed out of place in this cramped, greasy spoon restaurant. Yet awakenings take place in the mundane, not in the extraordinary. In the little minutes, the quiet minutes, great answers can be heard. Words are only symbols of what is beneath.*

# THE GRACE OF
# SPIRITUAL DEATH

#### ❧ ☙

DIVINITY:

*The gem I could not see*
*while the tumbling box of life polished my edges,*
*but which is now crystal-clear.*

Grief is the time when we are blessed with the opportunity to complete a natural process of spiritual death and rebirth before our own death. Other cultures describe the necessary steps of confession, conversion, and confirmation of the spirit before the actual death journey of the soul is completed.

In grief, we are put through, albeit seemingly prematurely, the dying process, long before we think that we are ready. For grief is a spiritual death while still alive. Frightening as this sounds to the Western mind, cultures rich with ancient knowledge have held this time as a sacred period of enlightenment. *Satori* is the Zen word for awakening from spiritual death. It is a goal in Zen Buddhism that the self should die, so that the true nature of the soul can emerge. Nowhere in our Western, TV-crowded minds can we make sense of this. We worship the SELF. We have magazines devoted solely to SELF. We go to therapy to get our SELVES back. Naturally, when grief pummels the SELF to death, we are panicked, afraid, and often seemingly insane.

In the immediate aftermath of death, all that we valued and believed is challenged. A new paradigm imposes itself on ours, and nothing seems to make sense about the world any longer. Perhaps that is because it is precisely the SELF, in capital letters of the Western mind, which interferes with spiritual fulfillment. When that SELF becomes merely self, relegated to its rightful place the background of our lives, a strange divinity rushes in. A flower can make us cry for its sheer beauty. A warm gesture from another is fully received and heartfelt. Contentment is found in what we used to think of as boring or nonproductive times. What we have labeled unimportant takes on new meaning.

So often, we see grief as a tragedy, when it is in fact a divine gift not everyone receives before their own death. Ironically, we are very lucky to live the rest of our days out with a new appreciation for what is truly important in life.

If there is a gift for us in exchange for our losses, it is a new, constant state of cherishing.

⁂

*I knew then and know now that all it would really take to die is to let go. The caliber of faith, the velocity of releasing, the capability of dying of my own free will is very real to me. I watched my mother let go and slip away, when then and even now I believe she could have held on. I had hated her for the choice she made. Hated her for leaving me. After you died, I finally understood her choice. I am at that ledge where the choice is offered. I am carrying another life, but the choice is still mine.*

*I cannot say that it was actually my will that has kept me from choosing to go with you. I would like to think that I am a loving mother, that I had hoped for a child long enough that I could not simply cast off that dream. But I'm sure there is another, stronger will at work. If it were simply up to me, I think I would simply relax into death.*

*Dying seems easy. Living is hell.*

*Many months later . . .*

*I do think, in some strange way, Clio's will to come into this world was stronger than mine. She had fought hard to get conceived in my infertility. She bucked the odds and was conceived the very last time we made love. She has survived the death of her father and the utter spiritual destitution of her vessel/mother. She did not cry when she was born, but looked straight at me, and smiled. I felt the power of this little helpless baby, her thrust to live her life.*

*In the moments when I held her, the magical days afterward, I knew that all the Eastern religious doctrines in the world would not have convinced me that hanging onto the spirit of my dead husband had been the wrong thing to do. As a mother, I made a decision. No one would take by baby's life away. Not even me. And certainly, if I could not survive to bear her without holding you back from your journey, then that was simply the way it was going to be. A dead man for a live daughter. It was an easy choice.*

# HAIR SHIRTS AND
# OTHER PENANCE

❧ ❧

DERANGEMENT:

*Rituals that seem mad
from the outsider's point of view,
but from within make perfect sense.*

renetic and fragile all at once is a delicate state. In grief,
it is simply a form of inertia. One must make circles and
pace them out. If we did not, we might be turned to
stone, statues to the state of nonexistence.

Perhaps it is because there is no true inertia in the physical
universe—for matter is always in motion—that we invent fren-
zied activity in the all-too-still-ness of our life as it stands in
our loss. To become completely still is to go against nature.
Yet what is there to do but wait for the sanity to return?

What appears to be derangement from observers is only a
rearrangement of all parts of our personalities. Still, it seems
to be so deeply disturbing to watch. Those who loved us,
liked us, respected us, are watching a re-forming of a human
being outside of the womb. Since this has always been a pri-

vate domain, and since we are not concerned with what others think, our friends and loved ones watch in the kind of horror they would have if they saw us defecating in the middle of a boulevard. It is the saving grace of derangement that it has no cognizance or respect for the opinions of others.

*Three o'clock in the morning. The phone rings but I can't answer it. Can't say, "Yes, I'm fine" if it's one of my night owl friends checking in. I'd rather it was the obscene caller who got my name from the obituaries. Him I could hang up on. He doesn't want to know how I am. At least he's honest.*

*The basics are overwhelming. Eat. Can't eat. Eating means I have to go to the store and think about what to cook. Or going to a restaurant and risk being seen, eating alone. They'll give me that look. That pitiful, disgusted look, and they won't move. In fact, they'll pretend they didn't see me. I can't seem to shake the shame of losing you. Intellectually, I know there is nothing to be ashamed of. I didn't kill you—you died. But there is shame. Swallowing me up. I can't trust anyone because they all pity me. And I begin to wonder if pity isn't a way they defend themselves against the searing truth: People die. We die.*

*The stages of grief are a hoax. There aren't stages. Only waves of feelings two and three at a time. One day I tore up your picture. One night I slept with the pieces of that photo. For one month I wore your sweater, day after day, until your smell was gone and only mine remained.*

*Why do I live? Why? I ask over and over and over. Why did you die? I ask over and over and over. DIED. Died. died. I say it again and again to hear it, but it is just a word.*

# HOSTAGE TO DEATH

⚜

SUICIDE:

*The act of exercising the ultimate option*
*while leaving everyone behind*
*as hostages of guilt, shame, and rage.*

Suicide is the act of exercising perhaps the only option we can see. Why must we criminalize suicide, morally, religiously, and even legally, when at times it really may be the only appropriate response to agony? Those of us who have been deserted by suicide are left with the rage of that desertion. Those of us who have considered it have, if only for a brief moment, seen the ultimate sanity of it. Yet we don't want to give permission to a suicidal person. So there are laws against it. Serious laws that carry long prison sentences. What an irony that we should think to make suicide a felony with a long prison sentence—what an irony that we would punish people for having such pain and hopelessness that they see death as the only release! We are insulted by the terminally ill who choose to commit suicide rather than wither away, losing their dignity and bankrupting their families.

*89*

To be abandoned by the one you love by suicide leaves you prey to the moral onus that we have put on suicide. Whether it is true or not, we can look around at the accusing looks of our friends that reflect the guilt we feel inside. Without fail, the suicide survivors are abandoned by many. It is as if we were somehow a part of an atrocity against the very sacredness of life. More than anyone, we will know the ways we failed. More than any jury, we will sentence ourselves to the shame of reliving every moment to imagine how we could have changed something and made a different result.

Yet, under it all, the reality is that there was a choice made by the suicide that we had no power over. None. An honest probe into how this makes us feel will unleash the rage we have at the powerlessness. *How dare you choose to die!* It is the most denigrating form of rejection. And it is appropriate that it should arouse the deepest contempt a human is capable of feeling. Most of us left hostage by the act of suicide would like to kill that person ourselves.

Still, there is another level that we will get to after all the primary responses. We come to understand that a suicide is not a personal vendetta against us but a response to a profound spiritual dilemma. It takes a long time to come to respect the factors of mystery in our spiritual lives, even longer to become comfortable with living with such unknowns. Ultimately, it takes a sacred humility before the gods of the psychic realms, for we are small before those mysteries.

The hardest part is that we will never be able to ask the suicide *Why?*

*Not long after you died, a friend committed suicide. I was pushed back over the edge, back to the day you died. I spoke to him in the car, day after day, like I had spoken to you. One night, I parked at the lake and I yelled what I really felt at him.*

*I wanted to shake his limp body back alive—violently shake him. I wanted to kill him for killing himself. How could he! How could he reject me so vehemently? We were **friends!** What did I do to cause this kind of pain that he would not find it worth something to go another day? What **didn't** I do that made him feel so empty and desperate? What were the secrets he could not tell me? Was I so insensitive that I missed them? He took himself away from me. And now, what do I have? Oh, why couldn't we have discussed this first? Was our relationship so meaningless that he could not find even one single reason for staying?*

*"TALK TO ME, DAMN YOU!"*

*But just like you, husband, he wouldn't answer me.*

# " H o w   A r e   Y o u ? "

IMPATIENCE WITH THE LIVING:
*What I feel most of the time.*

This is the question a grieving person hates more than any other question. Ask it and we'll hate you. Don't ask and we'll hate you.

Those around us care, but they are caught between sympathy and the rude awakening that tragedy can happen so very close to home.

"How are you?" becomes merely a greeting for most, not a genuine inquiry. Sometimes we'll be able to resist the temptation to tell them the truth, and simply answer back "I'm fine," as if it were simply a wave hello. Other times, we won't be so strong.

*You don't want to know how I am. So when you ask, "How are you?" of course I'll say, "I'm fine." But I really want to say: "How the hell do you think I am? Do you want me to say I'm fine so you can breathe easier? So that you can go curl up in*

*bed next to your husband and forget that mine is rotting in the cold ground as I am rotting in my cold bed? So that you can pretend that my agony is somehow unique and not a universal experience? Not contagious?*

*"You want to hear me say I'm fine, because you can't bear to hear about the howl that blows out of every breath I exhale, and the gasp that is sucked in with every breath I inhale. But I am you.*

*"You! I am speaking to you! Do you realize that it may happen to you? One day it could be you, standing in black next to a casket, comforting those who don't know how to comfort you, only to go home to a house where the sounds of your life have lapsed into an intractable silence."*

# Inadvertent
# Isolation

❦ ❧

ADMIRATION:

*A method of distancing*
*used in dealing with "the widow,"*
*which only makes me feel more lonely.*

Admiration is a slippery foe. While we all wish to be
admired, we can find ourselves inadvertently further
distanced from people by it. Admiration tends to set
us apart, at the very time we most need to make contact. We
certainly can't control whether people want to admire us,
but we should see it for what it is—a distancing mechanism.
It appeals to our egos while it implies that we surprised our
admirers with behavior they approve of.

Being respected is very different from being admired.
Respect honors our individual process, while admiration
approves of it. None of us is here to please another. Pleasing
others is a way we distance ourselves from our inner voices.
Rather than sitting quietly so that we can listen to the voices
of our souls, we seek the voices of others. It is normal and

natural to want to belong. And for this, admiration is treacherous, because it appears as belonging, while it places us alone on a pedestal. We must not be seduced by it.

*Letter to Everyone:*

*Don't admire me for what I've done, how well I've done, how I've handled this year of mourning. Admiring me humiliates me. What? Are you surprised? Admiring me says that I lived up to your expectations, and that you're surprised I did.*

*Hidden in this is a demand that I do what you want, and the implication that I'm not really capable. Hidden in this is your relief that I wasn't a burden on you.*

*Don't admire me. I did what I did to survive. I did what I did not for your admiration, but for my own inner integrity. You may respect me. But admiration distances you from me, and I am lonely enough. Admiration demands that I not fall back for fear of losing my reward.*

*Accept me. Expect that I would have handled this year with grace and strength. Expect it gently. And if I fall back, if my rage disappoints you, please be my friend. Expect that I will do my best, and don't put out the markers that measure what best is. Accept that I will find this myself. Expect that I will live as close to love, respect, and honor as I can.*

# In Anticipation

HOPE/NO HOPE:

*The state of being I swing between,*
*like a pendulum over two destinations.*
*I must let go to hang on.*
*I must surrender to win.*

I f we could yell, uncensored, at the world, it would probably go something like this:

Don't try to give me hope, damn you! I know there is
no hope. None. Everything I once knew is obliterated.
Every molecule in my body is changing. I cannot leave this
moment to contemplate the future. Hope! I despise hope.
It strings me out like a junkie, removes me from the
moment where I sit, yes in utter desolation, but it is my
desolation. Don't take it from me! Don't try to cheer me
up, for you invalidate what I have just seen. We all hum
along in this life, thinking we've got a tomorrow. Thinking
we've even got some kind of control over our future. Then
*wham!* The universe broadsides us with other plans. Like a
Zen koan, I have had my "Ah-hah!" And you, who have

never contemplated the koan, you wish to tell me in your Pollyanna-ish ways, "It was meant to be . . . !" When did Cosmic Central make you privy to the mysteries of life? You stumble through; I know, part of you hates to see me suffer. But much of you can't stand to see what your suffering will someday look like. I am your precognition, the ghost of Christmases to come. If you deny me my pain, you send me into the darkness alone, ashamed. But I refuse to be ashamed for coming alive. It looks like I am dying, but I am more alive than I have ever been.

It doesn't take much horse sense to know that when you see a woman, perched on a bridge, ready to jump, you don't tell her to take a bubble bath and everything will be okay.

Although it looks and sounds like rage, it is not. It is our deepest selves, trying desperately to tell the rest of the world how it feels to be left so utterly and completely. If only we can scream it loud enough, the world might understand, might welcome us back, might show a glimmer of recognition—for these things are universal. We know this in our bones. And we know that others know it, too.

*Sometimes, when I am paralyzed, overcome with my hopelessness, I suddenly feel excited about something. It's a bizarre swing. I can't seem to tell anyone about this. It sounds crazy if I say it out loud. But inside, it makes a weird sort of sense. I don't even know what I am excited about. Like a traveler who is aware of every moment, every step, without being able to see*

*the clearing at the end of the forest he travels through, I have an anticipation of something. Deep inside, I seem to know what it is. But my conscious mind can't access the facts. Only the feelings. I feel hopeful. This is new.*

*Hope. No hope. Hope. No hope. Hope. Hope. Hope. Cynicism. There is no hope. For whom? For me? For the way things were, says the voice from deep inside. Ah. I think, No hope for what was—is there hope for what will be? There is only hope for the new me—whoever she is. Feelings of nondescript joy waft in, and I squint hard to see where they came from. What will give me hope? Where does it lie? There is no answer. I must only wait.*

*Later—months later. Yes, there was no hope for the old life I led. I was never again going to be your wife. I would not live in this house for long. I would not be able to complain about your insensitivity ever again. I would not have your priorities leading me as a dog is led on a leash, ever again. I am left to discover, to forge my own priorities. If my plans don't work, I can't blame anyone else. They will be my plans only. I am alone. It is overwhelming. I sleep all day and pace all night.*

# INK BLOTS

CORRESPONDENCE:

*What I do to reach myself*

*when I'm no longer home.*

Writing letters is a way that we can express a part of ourselves we can't seem to say out loud. Corresponding with those in the same situation is healing. We find ourselves unedited. We can bask in our freedom to say what we normally edit with "civilians."

Correspondence is also a ritual to keep in touch with the inner self. This is ultimately more important than appearing to be handling everything "okay."

We see our feelings clearer when they are in ink. Though all of these feelings are transient (for in all things, *this too shall pass*), they are mailed into the annals of our history-making, marking our progress, and including our correspondent in our process. Someday, we might see those letters as we comb over our past, and we will smile, for they are records of our milestones.

*Dear Widow Snell,*

*Tongue in cheek, I call myself the Widow Hinton with a small few who would get the joke. It has a nice cadence to it, and conjures up all kinds of images so paradoxical to my image of myself that I often laugh when I say it out loud. I hope calling you the Widow Snell will be taken in the same spirit, though I'm sure you've tried it on and it doesn't quite have the same cadence. Probably because the sound of Snell seems to want a period after it, and besides Snell rhymes with knell and I think of the old metaphor, "the death knell is ringing." However, it does seem to carry with it a wonderful ominous tone that would jolt a few out of a thought or two. For many, jolting is the only way to eke an authentic thought from them. So be it.*

*I loved your candor about the things people will or won't say, at the untouchableness of widows, at the brutal honesty of your friend's comment—"The good husbands always die." (If this is true, then honestly don't you sometimes wish he was just a good ole sonofabitch?) I love what you would say to the stupid comments said to the bereaved. Yes, Time is a brutal enemy and a gentle friend. When you talked about being in Montana, I cried. Yes, I, too, know how much of our husbands' greatness we begin to acquire. I, too, was married to a man of calm (though you were lucky that George's quiet was inside rather than outside).*

*Then you hit a rare and lovely metaphor—George putting up lights around the house, lights that warm you in the winter of mourning. For me, the lights went out. I eventually had to changed all the damned light bulbs. My metaphor, though* opposite yours, is still a metaphor for my life as yours is for your life. You're wondering if the dead feel anything is poignant. I, too, have the same questions. I listen to bluegrass music on Saturday mornings now, something I never did when he was alive. I, too, chant, "He's gone. Really gone." For me, strange things have happened and I can see that I avoid doing the male things around the house because it means he really is dead. He would have done those things. Your feelings of aging . . . ah, yes. Although I am ten years younger, death has made me feel what you have written—I, too, hold my head a little higher to avoid the loose skin under my chin. Your salty descriptions of the women you knew with chin hairs made me chuckle. I could feel how free you are from apologies. It's amazing how many years we worried about chin hairs when life was passing by. But then, who really knows what they've got until it's gone?

Keep rolling up the hoses.

Sincerely, Stephanie

# JUNK

MEANINGLESSNESS:

*All the things I valued in my life*
*that are now trivial.*

The blinders of our existence are ripped off and we see the mundane, the trite, the trivial with such clarity it either makes us nauseated, or makes us laugh. How naïve we've been. How naïve the rest of the world is. It's like putting on a new set of glasses: We're stunned at the garbage that cluttered our lives. The task of cleaning out the closets, throwing out the junk of our lives has begun. There is no turning back.

*My husband is dead. I've said that so many times, it feels more like a role that I'm rehearsing for a play I personally wouldn't want to see. Removed from all that was, I spend my days gathering up the remnants left from the blast of his death, discarding what is shattered, keeping only what is chipped. Those chipped and dented parts of my life will go in a drawer to be*

*fixed. The drawer where things live, waiting for glue and touch-up paint. It's ridiculous to think I will attend to them, ridiculous to think that someday I'll be whole again. Like all things that wait too long to be fixed, they will eventually turn into junk.*

# LABEL ME WIDOW

WIDOW:

*One more tiring label*

*that people can put on me,*

*which tells the world about my private life.*

Widow—black widow—the spider who has sex with a male and then kills him. Widow's peak—an eerie growth of hair over the forehead—Dracula's coiffure. Widow's walk—a lookout cupola on New England rooftops, meant to house the poor widow so she can bay at the moon for her sailor husband, lost at sea. Merry widow, who is glad her old dead-beat husband is gone, and his bank account isn't. Widow—an extra hand dealt in cards; a leftover word that makes paragraphs look silly. Widow—originally, it comes from a word meaning unwhole, dirty, separate.

It reveals so much. It pries into your past and announces your private affairs. It is like walking with a cane. It signals to people that you are different. It scares wives who live in shaky marriages. It makes single men fear that they are and always will be, second choice. It conjures up images of old women sitting alone in the dark, dressed in black. It erases your name from dinner party lists. It tells the world you are no longer a part of a whole. It makes you scary.

Widower, on the other hand, conjures up a very different image. Poor man, poor lost lonely man. On a statistical average, he usually remarries in a year. Men have fewer problems finding another woman—(after all, it's our "duty" to take emotional care of men ...) Whereas the widow, *if* she remarries, waits an average of ten years ...

*Labels are for cowards, small people who need to place you in neat little cubbyholes so you will fit into their beliefs. I hate being a widow. Sometimes I wear black just to scare people. Sometimes I speak of my late husband just to see them squirm. The word "widow" weighs me down. Men joke that they'd better be careful not to marry me if that is my luck with men. Somehow being a widow is* my *fault. Your dying is something* I *did. If I'd fed you better, kept you out of bars and well satiated in our bed, you'd be alive today. What bunk.*

# LAUGHING
# RESUSCITATION

HUMOR:

*The backside of agony.*

If we look at a photo of a person frozen in a laugh, we can
see how closely it resembles agony. Comedians will tell
you, privately, that the only really funny jokes are the ones
that stem from pain. Laughing is the dark side of hurting.
Laughing reforms the toxic infrastructure of agony so that
we can deal with it. It is more than necessary—it is vital.

Laughing creates a bond between us and others who share
the joke, which will wear better than understanding, empathy, sympathy, or counsel. It sets us free from false myths,
and restores twenty-twenty vision. Laughing is the Buddha's
way of reducing the universe to palatable, bite-sized pieces,
so that we won't choke.

The things we accept as normal, by virtue of collective
agreement, are often the things that make us laugh the hardest in our grief. The insanity of killing for peace—working
sixty hours a week for the freedom of owning our own

home—imprisoning ourselves in hostile families so that we have a sense of "belonging"—these are only a few of the ridiculous "beliefs" that we find hysterically silly in grief.

Laughing is our window into sanity.

✺

*The strangest, most morbid things make me laugh now. Joke: Why are there fences around graveyards? Answer: Because people are dying to get in. Joke: A millionaire is accosted by a mugger who says, "Your money or your life!" The millionaire doesn't answer. The mugger says, "Well, what'll it be? Your money or your life?!" And the millionaire says, "I'm thinking ... I'm thinking ..."*

*Headlines like this make me laugh:*

POLICE KILL MAN DURING SUICIDE TRY ...
*Police shot and killed a man during a struggle that ensued while they were attempting to keep him from committing suicide ...*

*Or the widows I laugh with. One of my widow friends has her husband's ashes in the trunk of her car. Occasionally she opens it up and says hello. It horrifies her friends, but she likes it—after all, he goes everywhere with her. When she opens her trunk for the grocery boys, she introduces them, "This is my husband, Fred." One day the urn spilled, mixing up with a broken sack of kitty litter. She simply scooped up the ashes, and more than a few pebbles of litter, and poured it back into the urn. "Well," she said, "he always was kind of a gritty guy ..."*

*It's morbid. Gruesome. And it's refreshingly real.*

*The night before your funeral, Julia took me out to dinner so we could be alone. Our house was full of people I wasn't even sure I knew. I wasn't sure about much. We sat down to eat, and she let loose with that scathing humor of hers. I couldn't stop laughing. She was relentless. She said everything I was afraid to admit I was thinking. I had to laugh. Howl even. And I thought, "Oh, my God, if someone sees me here, the night before my husband's funeral, laughing and looking like I'm having a grand old time, what will they think?" How could they know that I was in the midst of receiving mouth-to-mouth resuscitation ...*

# A LESSON

LOVE:

*A state I cannot say I understand any longer.*

Sometimes, love makes no sense. It is not reachable from any place in our wounded selves. It is a mystery, an enigma—reserved for others. As we piece the bits of our shattered selves back together, loving someone else is impossible. Who is there to love that someone? A mess of shards and broken bits of human being? How can we love if we are not whole?

This will pass. Stay where you are, for it will move through you, and loving will be as air is to a bird, as natural as breathing. You don't even need to believe this—you only need to trust it.

*What I know is separation. Departure. Rejection. Abandonment. Limbo. What I have wanted to know is communion. Intimacy. Falling backwards knowing there are arms to catch me. Trust. Will I ever have it again? I fear that I am inca-*

*pable of trust. I have not learned to trust for any significant length of time, or to practice letting go with another. To allow another person to love me.*

*I do know what some people don't know—that in the end, there are losses. Necessary losses, some call them. I have not come to this junction yet. I see them as losses, yes, and I have made the best of the situations. But I sit in self-imposed solitude, for I have learned that if I give too much of myself, I can lose. Is this part of loving? Losing is part of loving. Loving means losing. It's apparently part of the equation.*

# LIFE STOMPS ON AHEAD OF ME

CHILD:

*The life you left behind to keep me living.*

A widow friend wrote to me once, "Though I don't envy the loneliness of bearing your late husband's child, be grateful that you have someone to touch." The bed is cold for us. It will stay that way for a long time. Even when a lover comes to hold us, there is the shadow of the reality, hovering over the experience. You find yourself saying, "Tonight is lovely, but tomorrow night will be hell again." It is sometimes not even worth risking the relief of being gently touched, for the chill, the emptiness that we've become accustomed to, had grown bearable, and now it would be unbearable once again.

This widow made me realize the value of loving someone. My daughter slept with me in the first eight months of her life. I nursed her and we cuddled, and sometimes, most nights because I rarely sleep well, even now, two years later, I would simply lie there, breathing in her smell, relishing the softness and warmth of her little growing body, pacified by her angelic face and little stuffed-toy noises she made when she nursed.

And though I would not have my daughter for long in my bed, it was a time when she returned every bit of nurturing I was providing for her. It is not the job of a child to save her mother. It is only her job to eat, and sleep, and grow. But I was sustained by the miracle of her coos and suckling, her wet diapers and her nestling body. I would forever be grateful that she helped me through that time. So, I say to my friend, thank you for helping me stay grateful.

*To my late husband—*

*Clio is safe with me. I promise. I promise to nurture her, let her spirit soar, let her finger all the things in her small world. I promise to shelter her from danger when she needs it and to step away when she needs to find out for herself.*

*I've never been so fascinated with anyone or anything before. I am in awe of her. She is life, stomping forward. Through puddles, dragging me along with her sunflower face that lights up whenever I walk into the room. She is the flower that has no respect for the granite that covers her. She is an early evening star that points me toward a destination. She is the innocence that you would never let me see. She is the steel hand of God, gloved in giggles and quiet moments before bed. She leads me into the next day. She is the tiny piece of God I get to hold. The spirit I've been honored and entrusted with. She is pure amethyst, clear blue skies and gentle sea foam tickling my toes. She is the embodiment of love, in its most virginal, idealistic form, giving it, demanding it with no apology or fear. She is an undaunted enthusiast for the things we consider trivial and therefore cease to recognize in our self-important, grown-up lives.*

*The things only children and old people are blessed to appreciate, the important things of life, like the sound you can make by opening your mouth and patting your hand over it while singing or the fascination of an ant's frenetic journey up your leg, the smell of a dandelion, the feel of a cat's fur, the taste of cold.*

*She brings my world to a halt so I, too, can touch with my fingers, discover my toes, and see with my eyes. She is your beauty, left as a last-minute, good-bye gift, and like all the gifts you ever gave me, she was meticulously, personally, lovingly chosen. And exactly right.*

*Thank you, dead husband, for that night of intense love where you shoved at me all the past, present, and future debts you wanted to pay off. Thank you for giving me something to live for when it all seemed so pointless, thank you for reassuring me you were flesh and blood. Thank you for injecting me with not only a miracle but a life, a future, a direction, and purpose to keep on plugging away for when I would have rather gone with you.*

*In her, I look and see an exciting future, filled with love, broken hearts, worried nights, bursting pride, and gentle moments in summer dusks, swinging together on the porch swing.*

*Every day she moves forward, so do I.*

# LIFTING OFF
# THE MASK

FAÇADE:

*Our camouflage fatigues;*
*the mask we wear*
*to keep the world from knowing*
*who we really are.*

Never have façades been more transparent than now. Why do we insist on trying to hide from others? Why do I hide? Why did you?

The space left in loss wears no mask. No mask can disguise the emptiness of it. There is little time or use for masks in this life. They only waste our time, the precious little time we have together. Do we want to leave this world, knowing that no one knew us? Do we want to leave behind someone who will lament never knowing who was behind the veil? How can we ever know that we were loved if the face we wore was not our own?

*I walk toward the white slab of marble. "Hi, Baby ..." tumbles out of my mouth in the habit of my old ways with you. The diminutive I used for you, granite face, chiseled from your cheekbones to your soul. It was a strange nickname for you, so formidable in life. I don't think anyone else ever dared call you Baby. It was an oxymoron. You were the oxymoron. A contradiction of what I sensed versus what I heard. "You bastard," I used to say, "you're messing with my head now ..." (I used to ... I used to ... I say that a lot now.)*

*I hated your silence when you were alive. It signaled danger coming. And you used that silence to get me. To scare me. You knew I was afraid of it and its aftermath. You bastard. You liked scaring me, like the man behind the curtain. And when I pulled back the curtain to discover your thunder was machine-made, you repeated over and over, "Pay no attention to that man behind the curtain!"*

*But that man behind the curtain was my Baby.*

# THE LIGHT GOES OUT

DWELLING IN DARKNESS:
*The moments when I am healing*
*by succumbing to the depression.*

Few people who have not experienced deep loss can understand the bereaved's need to suffer. Suffering is cleansing. It is necessary. The isolation is mysteriously helpful and healthy. How long you must suffer depends on your own internal pain barometer. There is no prescribed time limit, no recommended allotment of angst.

Our grief is intensely private. There are no words to describe it, because words dwarf the experience. The things I said to my late husband in the months and even years after his death were between him and me. Sometimes, telling someone else is helpful, because talking into darkness is tiring.

Living on after the death of someone you loved is much more difficult than dying. This is not to shame those who let go and die soon after their spouse. Proving your strength by living on without fulfillment gives no one a badge of courage. But some of us have reasons to go on, even though we don't want to. For me, it was my child. I was responsible for bringing her into this world, and therefore, I owed it to her to stay alive. This obligation sustained me until I could live for me. It took a long time, perhaps over a year. But in that year of hopelessness that shrouded my days and prodded my nights, I did a sort of penance necessary to appreciate the life I have today. I did not do it for this. At that time, I had no idea I would love life so much today. I simply muddled through long enough until I healed.

*One by one, every light bulb in the house has burned out since you died. I walk into a room—hardly remembering why I'm there—flip on the switch, but there is only darkness. One by one, the light bulbs die. One by one, they disappoint me, stop me, remind me. You are dead.*

*I don't remember ever changing light bulbs in our house. Did you do it all the time? Now the darkness slowly enfolds me. I have stopped caring if there is light or if there is dark. Sometimes now, I even prefer the dark.*

# L I M B O

PURGATORY:

*A place where I am unable to grieve;*
*frozen-ness; the place where the living dead dwell.*

Perhaps the hardest losses are the most intangible—dreams, hopes, fantasies. What is intangible cannot be buried. No one gives a funeral for the loss of hope. Few letters of condolence come when we lose a dream. That which was left unfulfilled leaves us alone, to grapple with the question of why, over and over. We are in a constant state of limbo, unable to mourn. Unable to let go for fear of losing what little we have. Unable to move on with our lives.

A sergeant in the U.S. military wanted to spare a widow the grief of knowing her husband was dead. This sergeant, knowing that the army would cut off support for her and her three children, made the decision to label him missing in action, even though he had witnessed the man's death. For twenty-two years, the widow held a vigil for the man she believed would, one day, walk back through her door. She did not remarry. She stayed married to a corpse. She did not grieve. Not until the truth came out that he was dead.

Whether the sergeant did her a service or a disservice is difficult to say. The army supported the widow and her children until they were grown. But this family was not allowed to move on. They were left to float in the purgatory of limbo, afraid to grieve for fear it would actually cause his death, for fear of being disloyal to him if he was alive. The intentions of the sergeant were honorable. But a woman lost twenty-two years of her life for a measly pension.

*When I was seven, my father, who was an alcoholic, left one day for a pack of cigarettes and never returned. I did not know that he didn't want to cause us pain by staying with us. I did not know his intentions were honorable.*

*I waited. For years, in limbo, I waited for his return. I was not given the gift of an ending, a good-bye, so that I could stop hoping he would come around the corner one day. I feared even thinking that he was dead for fear of killing him. I could not grieve. I could only live those years in limbo.*

# THE LOOK ON PEOPLE'S FACES...

PITY:

*The rasp that opens my shameful wound;*

*the look on people's faces*

*when they haven't a clue what to say to me,*

*and when (I suspect) they want to believe*

*that it will never happen to them.*

Pity is debilitating. Don't accept it. Run from it. It sends us out to the fringe and we can never get back in. It seduces us when we are feeling sorry for ourselves. Self-pity is our personal right. But pity from others is a slap in the face of our competence, our strength, and our transformation. It is useful only if we want to lower ourselves to manipulating others to get what we want. It works quite well for this. But other than that, it serves no other purpose but to put a safe distance between us and them. Don't let them off the hook so easily. Stand on your own two feet.

*To my friends: When I hurt, or am afraid, or falter in any way, don't pity me. Like admiration, this, too, humiliates me. I am already humiliated by the helplessness of my loss. The shame of being a victim of tragedy is more difficult than the tragedy itself. Maybe this doesn't make sense to you. Maybe you disagree. But it is true. I am ashamed that Jim died. I am ashamed that his family abandoned me. I am ashamed to be left alone. I am ashamed, because I know these things elicit pity, and pity demeans me, dehumanizes me. Pity is a vote of no confidence. Accept me even if you can't understand me. Only in this way can I begin to reaccept myself.*

*Some say: "You must accept yourself first before anyone can accept you." This is utter nonsense. As if enlightenment could happen in a vacuum. This only sends me into the dark, further into shame. I need you. I need your unconditional, unquestioning acceptance. This is love. And this is the only thing that can convince me that I am worthy once again. This is the only thing, besides the acid passage of time, that can heal me.*

*(But who can give this? I need this impossible thing to be healed. But I can't get it because no one can give unconditional, unquestioning acceptance. So I can't heal. But I am healing. Healing, which is clearly mysterious, must also be truly miraculous.)*

# LOST POSITION

TITLES:

*The way we define ourselves*
*by association with someone*
*we are deeply connected to.*

We are altered by death. When our parents die, we are no longer children. No longer sons or daughters. Even if we are middle-aged when this happens, it is a shock. If our child dies, we are no longer a parent, even though we still feel like one. When our spouse dies, we are no longer "so-and-so's" husband or wife—and we are thrown into that purgatory of divorcées, though we did not fail our marriage.

If we're newly married, we receive less deferential treatment, because "after all, you weren't together for long...." If our spouse held a popular or powerful position, we see how much it defined us, both in our own minds and in the society as a whole. If we were married to deadbeats, we are sprung from their reputation as well. And if there was no "formal" association, like marriage, we will see others treat us with less regard than we deserve.

Fiancés and live-in partners are perfect examples. There is no established role that gives us permission to grieve as deeply as we feel. Often, the loss of a fiancé or our life partner is more devastating than the loss of a husband of fifty years. The hopes and dreams, the plans, everything that was to be, collapse. Even if it would have turned out terribly, we will never know.

Legally, too, this is reinforced. Fiancés and life partners are reminded of their lack of rank from the choosing of the casket to their place in the funeral procession. They fall through the cracks. Their grief is dismissed. This is blatant cruelty, cruelty that our society fosters by its subtle instructions and invisible rules.

※

*"Fiancés aren't shit." Steve laughed. His eyes howled from tears fallen, from tears yet to fall. "I found that out when she died. We ain't shit, not emotionally, not financially, not legally." He laughed again, like a cough. "But it doesn't matter." I walked behind him through the sculpture garden that was once a city dump. "When I got back from South Carolina, my buddies had made this memorial for her." I looked through the weeds and saw a little white bench facing a flat stone, already crowded by the grass that grew up around it. He coughed again. "Yeah, look, there's her name—spelled wrong, but what the hell, man, it doesn't matter."*

*Surrounding the bench and stone, a wrought-iron cord hung, sculpted to look like it draped over iron posts. The bench faced the street, a wide, industrial part of town. A chain-link fence separated the sidewalk from the memorial. Here he sat, mostly in the middle of nights, baying at a moon that had eclipsed on him. Three weeks before they were to be married, she was knocked off a pontoon during a wedding party, and crushed by a speedboat. The driver had been drunk. Steve had watched the whole thing.*

*I cannot imagine what pictures haunt the screens of his mind—of red in water, of the delicate flesh he had made love to pulverized. I met him three months after her death. I knew this would be his hardest time. Now, when his friends wear pained expressions because he talks so much about her. Even I could feel a part of me wanting to back away from him. He was living with a dead woman and he would do this for a while. As uncomfortable as it was to watch, he was working things out ...*

*He was practicing his new reality, constantly referring to her in the past tense. It takes a lot of talking to get it down. He had to practice, moment to moment, being alone. Burying the dreams of what might have been, putting her to rest so that someday there will be an empty place next to him to be filled by someone.*

*Until then, the shoes of this dead woman are too big for anyone.*

# MACH 1 AWAKENINGS

SPIRITUAL AWAKENING:

*A blinding flash of darkness*

*that launches me into enlightenment*

*seemingly without any choice on my part.*

To awaken is violent. Like the pilot who pushes out the envelope, defying the limitations of air resistance, he must penetrate the sound barrier to get to Mach 1. As the speed resists the steel of his plane, threatening to tear it up like Kleenex, the pilot must press forward. The roar, the shaking of the plane scream at him that he is a fool. The centrifugal force pins him back into his seat, freezing him like a bug in resin. But he keeps his hand on the stick, chanting, "This, too, shall pass." He keeps the moment of breakthrough in the front of his mind. At a certain point, he cannot turn back. To do so is to stay too long in the barrier and be destroyed. Then there is a moment when the violent shaking lessens, and he knows he has begun to penetrate the other side.

As he pierces the sound barrier, the sound vanishes. The great *BOOM!* heard on the earth below signals his penetration. He is launched into speeds he never dreamed possible—a projectile of steel flesh and human soul. It feels like nothing he ever imagined—there is little or no resistance. The sun looks like it is seven feet in front of him. The heavens are within touching distance. The sky is his home. Simultaneously, there is jubilation at the miracle of it and awesome terror of the loneliness.

I have never flown Mach 1 in an airplane, but I have flown it in my soul. Neither the pilot nor I will ever be the same again.

The experience up there, in the sky, is shared by few on the ground. There is a temptation to believe that it never happened. So it is with healing from death. The day I am changed forever will fade. The flash of illumination that simultaneously lit up and blacked out everything priceless and trivial will dim. Life demands that the trash be taken out, the grass mowed, that the mundane be attended to. In order to function, I will forget, just a little, about going Mach 1.

We cannot stay in the awakening too long without impairing our abilities to function in life. The danger here is that we can forget, wipe from memory, like an amnesiac, the experience, and settle back into the droning rhythm of life. The experience can be forgotten if it is allowed to be. There is little in everyday life that confirms it even happened. Logic wants to get rid of it, because it defies the natural order that logic tries to impose on us. I must make a conscious decision to keep the experience I have been gifted with—to remember all things about that experience, painful or not.

*Within this small window of opportunity, this quickly closing window, I choose to remember the moment when I heard you died, and I was launched into the sound barrier.*

*To continue to remember that moment, those days and months, means embracing the pain. It means that I now walk through this life with the eyes of a dead man joined to the eyes of a living woman, forever ready to see what should be honored, respected, and cherished. The pain, the loneliness is a small price for this new vision.*

*I hope the aching will subside and I will be left with the ability to see miracles in dandelion fluff, in the squirming of worms through mud, in the squeal of joy from my daughter's lips, in the soft, summer nights on the porch of my new home.*

*Instead of thinking that your death was solely a tragedy, I now see it as one side of a coin. The opportunity to experience being alive is the other side of that coin.*

*My husband, my friend, my lover, I loved you very much. I know that you have stood, and do still stand, next to me as a friend of lifetimes.*

# M~~ARRIED~~

❦ ❧

WEDDING RING:

*The circle that joins us;*

*the symbol that I belong to someone;*

*the only link I have now to you.*

When is the time right to take off the ring? For months, I hung on to those rings, not only as a link to my husband, whom I was still unready to let go of, but also for the protection of it. I now belonged to nobody. But I had once belonged to someone. This was an important combat I made against the abandonment I felt, and the isolation I was in.

One of my widow friends took hers off within the first month, only to put it on the day she went in to buy a new car. "I'll be damned if I'm gonna let one of these slick sales guys take advantage of me because I'm a widow." I admired her for that humorous but realistic move. It happens a lot, in our time of vulnerability; the vultures come around for their fill.

I was amazed at the people who made calls to me after my husband died, chatty little conversations that tried to explore my financial status. I myself took a long drive to Florida with my daughter, and before I left, I put a ring on my wedding finger. There are some real dangers out there, and signaling to the world that somebody is in my corner is somehow a smart thing to do.

One of my widow friends went on a vacation with the women of her church, a fundamentalist group. Nervously, but courageously, she removed her rings before she left. The group let her know they were appalled. She was, after all, eternally married to her late husband. Although it meant she had to find a new church, where they supported her going on with her life (which was no small loss to her, by the way), the time had come for her to move on.

Wedding rings are a dilemma for the widow and widower. They tell the world your heart is still with the person who died. And during the time when this is true, wearing the rings is an important gesture. After all, we are not divorced! We did not choose to lose our spouses. We had no say in this event whatsoever. We were married, and then we weren't. There was no ceremony, no legal proceeding, nothing that marked the passage into the new life we were forced to live. But there comes a time for most of us when we no longer want to drag a dead body around with us. When the empty space next to us is filling up with our new sense of self. When we want to invite a new person into our lives. And there is no place for our late husbands and wives.

*I play with the ring you put on my hand that glorious day in June so many years ago. I twist it round and round until my*

*finger is raw, and I welcome the small physical pain that barely counters my great interior pain. I wonder, when do I take this off? I'm not married now. I found that out today when I filled out a form that asked me to check one of two boxes: Single? Divorced? The word widow is so feared it isn't there. I am not single. I am still married to you until I decide that I am not! I will decide this. I wrote in the word widow and drew a little box. In this I take control.*

*I had no control when you made me into a widow. I didn't do anything to deserve this. I didn't cause a divorce. Nor did I want one. I married you, for better or for worse, in sickness and in health, in life and in death. I need to stay married for now. I need to keep your protective circle around my finger. Not to show people that I am a good widow, or that I was a good wife, or that I am properly in mourning. Not that I need to tell the nonexistent hordes of men just waiting at my door to beg for my hand in marriage. Hah! But because I need to maintain some minuscule delusion of having control over my life.*

# MEMORY CRACKS

AMNESIA:

*The ritual of my unconscious
sorting out what is important
and what is not important,
what is tolerable
and what cannot be survived at this point.*

rief does strange things to memory. Some things are blacked out entirely. Some things hide until we are strong enough to remember them. Some things just go, for no apparent reason. There are people we've met whom we cannot remember meeting. It is curious. Perhaps it comes from a mysterious reordering of time and priorities. When loss throws us into the cold theater of reality, where we are forced to see, in black and white, what is really important versus what we thought was important, the memory banks are refilled.

Sometimes we block out what we cannot survive remembering. This is a different sort of amnesia. Things too horrible for our current level of strength evade us. They will evade us until the time comes when we are ready to remember. And though the act of remembering can seem like a searing brand on tender flesh, it is survivable when it comes. Our higher selves know better what we are ready for, and when we must face what keeps us static. This higher self knows we are strong enough. Like a pregnant woman who cannot imagine surviving her labor pains, we may try to dodge the pain. But, like the pregnant woman, there is no escape. She cannot, no matter how much she wants, get up from the labor bed and leave for a break. And though she thinks the next pain will kill her, it does not.

*In my second day of labor, I told Mary, my dear friend and birthing coach, "I can't do it any more! I can't! I really can't. I'm not lying!"*

*She looked at me, held my face three inches from hers, and said, "Oh, yes you can! And you will!" And I did. For that, I am forever changed. I got through my own self-imposed limitations. Once again, I was humbled by how little I really knew.*

*I remember the labor pains. Though they have dimmed. I remember when I heard you were dead. But the pain has become foggy. We really do get to forget once the pain has served its purpose.*

# MERCILESS LANGUAGE

*❧ ❧*

WORDS:

*Those bites of communication*

*that others use about us,*

*which serve to perpetuate*

*their misunderstanding*

*about the effects of grief.*

he words used about those of us who grieve tend to mean little to us. Surely the language is not one that we ourselves would use to describe our internal process. Words like "widow" seem foreign and decaying. Through historical redefining, it has come to be associated with images of bony fingers and black shrouds. Even the color black, which in many other cultures means protection, and even wholeness, our society relates to shadowy meanings and depressive symbols. The irony of this lies in the fact that black is the only color that contains all the colors of the spectrum. So it is with this place of grief. It contains the spectrum of emotions.

On the other hand, what is the word for a lover who has

lost his mate? Or the parent who has lost a child? Widow, widower are convenient labels, for they say all that another would need to (or want to) know about us. But for the mother of the dead child, we force people to speak the tragedy. Still, which would we choose? To be branded with the associations of words like "widow" or have no label at all?

Michel Foucault wrote in his book *Madness and Civilization* that madness is mute, a language of silence. And "As for a common language [between the "madman" and the "psychiatrist"] there is no such thing." . . . "The language of psychiatry, which is a monologue of reason about madness, has been established only on the basis of such a silence."

So it is with grieving. As in madness, grief has a deafening silence. As in madness, the world within is inexplicable.

The most insidious side of the language of grief is the *lack* of words that give weight to the experience. Those who chose to give us condolences seldom stop to recognize the power of the awakening that we are forced into. Instead they pity us, safely distanced from the heat of our experience. Unfortunately, few are willing to walk into the darkness before it is their time. If we try to tell others what it is like, we are stuck with words that don't even come close—*lonely*— *I am lonely now.* "Ah," they can say, "I know what that feels like." But they do not know this caliber of loneliness. It is like calling a hurricane a mere storm. There is just enough truth to cause a serious misunderstanding.

Moreover, the internal transformation that grief causes is messy. Sometimes even violent. We are open wounds that eyes turn away from. Few recognize that psychic surgery is being performed before their eyes. And most would prefer that this surgery take place under blue gowns in private surgical rooms, where the blood and the visceral matter of the soul is hidden from conscious awareness.

We, however, have little choice. We can succumb to this metamorphosis, often losing friends and additional loved ones along the way. Or we can cooperate with our culture's need for us to grieve with "dignity," as the nation watched Jackie Kennedy do. She was no fool. She wasn't about to expose herself to the lack of understanding and language about her situation. Like many of us, she withdrew into her private domain, to feel the avalanche of reality tumbling around her.

People want to understand. Yet those of us in the midst of grief know that unless they have been there, too, there is no bridge for them to walk across. There are only demeaning words of comfort.

*I can't find the words anymore.*

# Mists of the

# Ferryman

TRANSITION LOVER:

*A person who took me across the gulf*
*between your death and my life.*

Our first attempt out into the dating world will be
terrifying. And maybe even exhilarating. Somewhere, with someone, we will be ferried over into
the next way of life. At some point, we will take our clothes
off for another lover.

It can be such a pivotal experience that gratitude can make
it seem like it's true love. We are like children, who think
that every growth spurt is their last.

But this is just the beginning.

*I felt like a virgin. I felt like a cheating wife. I wanted to push*
*him away, but my body said to go. Then I thought I was in*
*love with him. But I was just grateful to be touched again.*

# Moving Day

NEW LIFE:

*Something that does not feel familiar to me,*

*but I know will slowly,*

*imperceptibly,*

*embed itself in me*

*as new saplings establish themselves in new soil.*

So we begin a new life. Chapter one. If only it felt as easy as it sounds in books. Should it be a new house? Another city? The Peace Corps? The choices are exciting and frightening at the same time. Sometimes we don't change a thing, at least on the outside.

Everything is different now, so nothing feels as easy as it was before. But we've stopped looking for "easy" a long time ago. Now we build a new history, a new set of memories that will grease our lives again someday, so that we won't have to learn where the grocery store is, we'll simply drive there. Until then, we walk new ground every day, feeling like guests in our own lives. Memories feel like all we have left.

But someday, today will be a memory, too.

*Moving day. Can't sleep. Up at four o'clock, dreaming, letting go. Today, this house we made a home has become a house again. The boxes are packed and moved. The furniture we carefully picked, loved, argued over, and collapsed on at night is in the truck. I wash the floors, the crumbs from the cabinets, the mice chewings from the drawers. I wash and wash, until the moment comes when the movers have gone and I am alone. The shell of this home remains. I look around. I've removed every trace of us for the new owner. But we are still here, in the air, in the walls. The four years of our lives together are soaked into the thirsty sheetrock like permanent paint. They can be covered maybe, but never removed.*

*The lazy days of winter when you were restless for your yard work, the busy days of summer when you couldn't keep up with the weeds. The croquet parties. The Sunday mornings when I used to catch you conducting Mozart on the deck. The vegetarian experiments you always complimented even when dinner was fit more for rabbits than humans. The late-night fights (always at night! or on Sunday!) over whether or not you were going to talk. The lovemaking. The infertile days of pressured sex when you refused to let science control our intimacy. (God bless you!) The wedding reception in the backyard when you looked so debonair and handsome I thought I'd burst out of my dress if I looked at you too long. Our worst fight, over whether we should have one or two parking lot attendants for the wedding.*

*All these moments fly through the house like bits of electrical energy, neutrons trying to put form to the intangible body of our relationship. You slip through my mind. Or is it the house?*

*The air next to me? Like a fish in a clear stream, invisible but ever-present, ever-powerful, ever-loving.*

*Now today, I leave here. I am not alone as I leave. I have had you. Few ever did. Maybe none. You gave me your genes to remember you by in Clio. I leave here with her, and also with enough memories to ward off self-pity.*

*It's ironic that my last night in our home is Valentine's Day—the day you always forgot.*

# NEITHER HERE NOR THERE

TRANSITION:

*The moments, strung out over months,*

*where I know I am no longer the woman I was,*

*but not quite the woman I am becoming.*

In the beginning, we are concave with the emptiness of our loss. To the outside world, we still look intact. We have arms and legs, a torso, a voice, a face. But this is only an illusion.

Perhaps it is the illusion the world wants to see. Perhaps it is an illusion we want the world to see of us. But if one could really see what a body looks like when hit with the meteor of loss, one would see an inverted body. A black hole. A reversal of the tangible energy into a whirlpool of pain, folding in on itself. In the beginning, we know who we are missing.

But later on, there is a forgetting. What we once knew so intimately eludes us. We have a hard time remembering the face of the person who died, or the voice of the one who left us. We feel only an empty space next to us. At night, we face our beds, and crawl into that empty space, knowing our dreams will waft through us, and us through them. We ache for one more encounter with the one who is gone, even if it is only in our dreams. We are beginning to forget the curve of the nose, the dimples in the cheeks, the expressions we thought were indelibly stamped in our memories.

Sleep will not be restful, for we no longer have a grip on what it is that we long for. We are in a seemingly perpetual state of longing, without knowing for what.

All things pass. Even pain.

*It isn't that depression is so terrible. That I can deal with. It is the loneliness. I don't want to be with anyone and I don't want to be alone. When I have a date around he takes up space. Sure, the loneliness is gone for a while, tucked away, but the space around me is crowded.*

*It isn't a fair trade-off.*

# A New Union

CONTEMPLATING ANOTHER RELATIONSHIP:
*The result of finally realizing*
*that I have something to give*
*someone, someday.*

The healing is slow. Solitude is often saturated with a belief that we will never love again and never be loved again. Replacing our loved one seems impossible. And it is. We can never replace him.

Yet if we are true to our grieving process, we will find ourselves changed. When we contemplate this new relationship, we won't be replacing but we will be reentering. Once our shame of the helplessness of our situation has healed, and the loneliness transformed into solitude, we know how much we have to offer. This is the ultimate kind of healing, for there was a time when we were certain we had nothing to offer anyone.

*And I am changed. I am changing. Now I don't miss you every second of the day. Now I only feel lonely for what we had.*

*Not so much for you. Now I only long for another person who will believe in me the way you did.*

*Loneliness is a snap. Stood up next to angst, torturous nights, endless emptiness, it's a cinch. But it is always with me, like a shadow. Yet I find myself whistling with a serenity I never had before. I can even imagine that I might be desirable someday, and that I might desire someone new someday.*

*One of your friends told me today that he felt sorry for the next man in my life. He said it would be different if I had divorced you. It would have meant I didn't want you. To be a widow, he insisted, meant that the next man would feel like he was always second string. I laughed at him. His insecurities were showing. He was telling me more about* him *than he was about me.*

*If any man feels that way, he's missing the point the way the untrained eye would fail to recognize a precious stone before it was cut and polished. This is the new strength in my vision.*

# ON MY OWN

EPIPHANY:

*The moment I realized*

*he was never coming home again.*

It isn't a new concept that a woman would find herself alone. There is nothing extraordinary about being alone. Or about being a woman alone, or a mother alone. In our culture, women often find themselves alone. Some moan and complain about the bastard who left them. Some courageously choose to be alone. Some find themselves waiting for the prince who has lost his white steed, and they are alone for a lifetime.

It is very strange that we pity the woman who is alone while we envy the man. As women, we've been taught since we had toys that we needed another to be whole. We were trained to catch men, from Barbie dolls to high school proms. It was the way we exercised the only power we were taught to claim. It is a great shock to learn that the story doesn't end with *happily ever after* at the altar, and the men who were supposed to be our heroes were often more fallible than our Ken dolls.

There are spurts of growth in life. Maturity happens after these spurts. Losses are only spurts in disguise. They are the backing up to leap forward. Most of us lose parents, jobs, friends, lovers. Most of us experience losses of all sorts. After the loss heals, we forget the acid moment of true vision, but only our conscious mind forgets. Our unconscious drives us forward, if we are willing, to the next level of maturity, never forgetting the vision.

*The notion of alone has a new context now for me. "On my own" is the way it has echoed through my dreams as I sleep. "He's dead and you're all alone" is what inevitably goes through my head when I'm confronted with tasks that I probably could learn to do. I'd much rather faint and turn them over to a savior kind of guy. Drill a hole for a screw to mount the towel rack? "I'm sure I couldn't," I can hear myself say, Scarlett-like. I resist. Mow the lawn when I can't yank the cord hard enough? I really need a man or at least a teenager in the neighborhood who will.*

*I'm so full of shit as a feminist. I wouldn't admit these things in certain female circles.*

*Yet there is a dimension of this "on my own" stuff that I know is damned real. Who is going to shout with equal glee when Clio stands for the first time? Who will share the worries about the money? No, it's my concern for the rest of my life, and there is no one here to worry with me.*

*I remember times when I wanted to be back "on my own" during our marriage. When it was hard, when changing into a "functional" intimate relationship seemed like trying to move a dead elephant. Times when I wanted to write without the intrusion of another person to be concerned about. I was only human. I am sure all wives and husbands have their moments, perhaps months or even years, of wishing they were back on their own, as they take for granted the tiny, invisible comforts the other person gives them. Few of us are prepared for the loss of those comforts. It is common. I do not lament that I was human. I do not lament anything today. I only reflect on how little I really knew about being on my own.*

# ON PRECIOUSNESS

LOVING:

*It's what I give that sustains me.*

*When I get it, it's just a lovely bonus.*

ove is the sole possession of the lover. The love of another can be taken away, by death, divorce, rejection, or betrayal. But the love that we feel for someone cannot. It exists inside of us and is an expression of who we are. Likewise, the love others feel for us is their expression. We can be stripped of possessions, titles, influence, and love of others, but no one can take what is within us.

Surely we enjoy, even bask in the love that others feel for us. As humans we need that love. Not to define us. Not to give us worth. But to help us feel a part of something. Still, in truth, we need to love more than we need to be loved. It is in that expression of love that our fulfillment blossoms.

*I've become aware recently that loving sustains me. It is so easy to love a child. I've never loved anyone the way I love my*

*daughter. It is a pleasure to give, and watch her take, unabashed. I expect nothing in return. I find reserves of patience I never dreamed I had. All she has to do is burp and I chuckle about it the rest of the day. I ask nothing of her, except to be healthy, to take, to grow, and I give all that I can to her.*

*It is loving that has healed me, not being loved. Not searching for a white knight to make me feel better. My own sole act of loving seats me firmly in the human race. It takes the edge off my despair. It allows me the dignity of not desperately seeking to find a someone to fill your place. Being loved is something I can wait for. But loving can begin with me alone.*

*Once, a long time ago, a woman said to me, "What other people think of you or feel about you is really none of your business." I now know she meant that what people think or feel toward me is more a reflection of what is inside of <u>them</u>, not a comment on me. I can see that the things I like or dislike in some people are often the things I like or dislike the most in myself.*

*So I think often about love. I think about my love for you. And yours for me. And I realize the most amazing thing: My love for you was mine, and your love for me was yours. No one, not even you, can take my love away from me without my consent. It is my business, not yours, that I loved you. It is your business, not mine, that you loved me. And when you died, you took all the love that was inside of you with you. And I've kept all the love I had inside of me. You will no longer hold me. No longer kiss me or write me funny little cards. And I will no longer cook for you, make love to you, or see you nodding off on the couch. All that is gone. What remains of your love is only a shadow. Not the love itself, just the memory of it. Your love is on its way to heaven. Or hell, or another life. Or wherever we go. It goes with you. It was never my possession. It was only a gift from you.*

*All those years, I wanted you to love me before I wanted to give my love to you. I dismissed my own love for you, even withheld it until I knew for sure you loved me. I had the whole equation wrong. I had no control over whether you loved me or not. I could not* make *you love me. Nor could I make you* not *love me. You would or you wouldn't. And, really, it had more to do with you and what was inside of you than it did with me.*

*I could never do enough to earn anyone's love. All my life, I tried to earn the love of others—by being smart or witty or pretty or especially charming. I concentrated on their love for me, and missed out on the benefit I would have gained in loving them. It was self-centered in a very deep way.*

*Now that I know this, it has become bearable that I did not get a chance to say good-bye. You knew that you loved me. I knew I loved you. Death cannot take that away.*

# Opening Again

LOVING AGAIN:

*The risk I am finally willing to take,*
*knowing so well that one day*
*I may lose again.*

When we begin to love again, we look back on the times when we were certain we would never again love or be loved, and we smile. How could we have been so blind? Yet it's the memory of those times that makes loving again so much more meaningful. We have more to give than we ever had before. We can receive more than we ever could before. And now, so acutely aware of the risk we take in loving, our love becomes more precious a gift than the love we gave with reckless abandon. Cherishing is the natural state of loving, and now that comes easy for us. The fear of losing haunts us sometimes, but we've been through the worst, and survived. It gives us a new freedom. We know that we may not be here tomorrow so we'd better love for all we're worth today.

*The outcome was death.*
*No, not the end, but the circle's*
*reinstatement of itself.*
*I shed my skins*
*As I take you inside of me,*
*You penetrate my mask and*
*Caress my inner sanctum,*
*The psyche of my hidden self*
*You claim without hesitation,*
*Before I am on guard for invasion.*
*Gently rising, rising,*
*Into me,*
*You thrust softness into me*
*With your hardness*
*And I am watery worlds*
*Wafting on silken clouds of*
*Timeless union.*
*My tears are for the shadows of*
*All the fears I have swallowed,*
*Ignored, or brushed aside,*
*Shadows falling like dominos*
*Into my joy.*
*I cannot have you without* not *having you, too.*
*I cannot feel your love without feeling what it is like*
        *without your love.*
*Bittersweet, my tears fall,*
*As I give myself to you.*

# OPPOSING PLACES

PARADOX:

*The two opposing places I straddle,*

*between which a fine line of light emerges,*

*and I begin to understand.*

Somewhere between the opposites of death and life is a place of odd and profound comprehension. Grief places us between yesterday and tomorrow, between what was and what is yet to be. We are caught, unable to move in either direction, unable to make sense of the paradox. There is no other choice but to wait and allow what will happen to happen. No amount of resistance or fight changes the unyielding fact of death. No amount of logic explains its ambiguities.

In time, a pinpoint of light flickers and waves to us. We chase it because we know that the waiting is over. Nothing will ever be explained in the way we first wanted—death still won't make sense to the person we once were. Instead we acquire a new context for the old facts—one that holds the contradictions in a precarious but meaningful balance.

Then a moment comes. Ever so quietly. Our inner conflicts are dispersed throughout a new tapestry of acceptance.

We have been slain by the dragon, and we have slain it in turn. All other dangers now seem puny in comparison.

*I stand at the tail of the dragon. No, I think I am standing at the mouth of the dragon. Which do I say first, "My husband is dead" or "I'm having a baby"? I have discovered where the circle begins and ends. I cannot look back without looking forward. The tail of death wiggles its way to the jaws of life. And I stand at the very point where the vacuum behind me has been neutralized by the vacuum in front of me.*

*I don't understand it with my mind. But I understand it in my heart.*

# PERENNIAL
# MELANCHOLY

DEPRESSION:

*A state I sink into which I do not notice,*

*like a fish does not notice water;*

*a necessary state of suffering*

*that does not endeavor to enlighten*

*but rather to force surrender.*

Chronic depression sounds like fly paper. Like mildew in a dank basement. It sounds like a car that refuses to start. It feels like forever. Actually, it means "born with a deficiency in endorphins." Those things that buffer us against the hard edges of life. Like diabetes means "born with too much blood sugar," or left-handed means "born with a better grip on the uncommon side."

Neurotransmitters—the little adhesives that put two and two together to get four. In chronic depression, two and two equal five hundred. Mellow people have a lot of serotonin. Highly intelligent people seem to have less serotonin. They know too much to be happy. Norepinephrine helps people roll with the punches of the world. Some of us aren't good rollers, and we stagger back into the ring for the fifteenth round. Some people can get up and brush themselves off after losing their jobs, and the next day they're out pounding the pavement again. Some of us die over a parking ticket. It seems just as serious.

William Styron, in *Darkness Visible: A Memoir of Madness,* says,

> The madness of depression is, generally speaking, the antithesis of violence. It is a storm indeed, but a storm of murk. Soon evident are the slowed-down responses, near paralysis, psychic energy throttled back to close to zero. Ultimately, the body is affected and feels sapped, drained. ...

It is not possible when the psyche is being destroyed and born again for the body to do anything but move like a slug that has just had salt poured on it.

*So I have considered those little pills, antidepressants. What would life be like without suffering? It's the wellspring of my work, the fuel injection of my search for answers. Yet I think about my child, so young, so deserving, and I think that if I have to be a less insufferable writer so she'll be a whole person who had a mother present for her, then I'll just have to make my writing calmer and my motives more contented. There is no trade-off in this transaction. She is the most important.*

# PISSING ON
# YOUR GRAVE

RECLAIMING MY SELF:
*The act of standing up to my dead husband,*
*and saying that I won't tolerate the pain any longer*
*by avoiding the negative feelings*
*I feel about him*
*because he isn't here to defend himself.*

The dead don't have to clean up their own messes.
They don't have to straighten out the late bills, the
lost wills, the floundering business investments.
They don't have to finish hanging the wallpaper they started
and left as a blaring reminder that they are gone. They don't
have to explain their irresponsible actions, their secret stashes
of pornography, or why they didn't keep their promises.
They don't ever have to take out the trash again, hang the
storm windows again, worry about money again, or mow the
lawn. They are off the hook. Goddammit.

*I had a plan. It came from my anger at you. My combined anger at your leaving, at promises made that you never kept, at dreams unrealized, at secrets I found out about you after you'd died. I was more than angry. I wanted to vent it, wanted to inflict it, wanted—needed—to thrust it out at you so I could claim back my heart. My grief counselor asked me, "What would you really like to do?"*

*I remembered how our dog had strutted straight to your grave, one among the many in your section, and lifted his leg on the mound of new dirt. I wanted to do that. I wanted to piss on your grave with the matter-of-fact attitude of our dog. I wanted to tell you that you can't treat me like this in life or in death. My counselor sanctioned my impiety with the shocking comment "That sounds like a healthy thing to do." I couldn't believe she said that. She, the ex-funeral director. The mortician. The beauty of a woman who had laid hands on thousands of dead people to make them presentable to the living. Now, as a consoler to the living, she was laying hands on my psyche to heal it. Pissing on your grave was "healthy." That was all I needed to hear. I didn't need to do it after that.*

*Then, one summer day, when the baby had been born, and I was picnicking on your grave, talking to you, telling you about her, I had to go to the bathroom. We were fully laid out, with picnic basket, diaper bags, lunch, and not a ladies' room to be found within a quarter of a mile. The baby was asleep in her infant seat. And I first thought of going to the little maple, and squatting, my skirt obscuring any flesh. But I* decided to sit on your grave. I pulled down my panties. The grass tickled. The ground was cool. And my trickle seeped in slowly, and I imagined it, working its way down, through the black dirt, down six feet, to the top of your vault, to pool on top of your dwelling place. It was the first time I had touched you in a very long time. The rage was gone. The love remained.

# QUIET PLACES

GRAVEYARDS:

*Peaceful places where all things are equalized,*

*where loneliness is the norm,*

*where, as one of the lonely,*

*I can contemplate without being pitied.*

Graveyards are for me. For the living. For the ones left behind. The people who need to go somewhere to touch the one who is now untouchable.

Walk the grounds alone, cry, even rant, and we will not get strange looks. Only the dead can hear it. They do not divulge our frailties. They do not remind us of how far we have strayed from "the norm." They do not comment. They only push up the tombstones, hold down the ground. And listen. They know.

The quiet of the graveyard pulls the secrets out of us. We can say what was never said. We can report how life is going without them. And there isn't pressure to get on with "our lives." Time in the cemetery seems nonexistent. Unimportant. Patient. The dead seem to know that we will someday heal. That our visits will become less frequent. But until then, they will tolerate our comings and goings, our soliloquies, and the mud we make with our tears.

*We put you under a small maple tree, a slab of white marble at the head of a mound that would someday even out with the rest of the grass. The chain-link fence was covered with winter-browned ivy stalks, bare so that I could see the lake through the thicket. It was a twenty-below wind chill that day we walked, tenderly, around the markers, to decide where you'd be buried. Someone said, "Good stiff breeze off the lake—he'll like that." And we even laughed. The cemetery "consultant" talked about the choices like he was selling vacuum cleaners door-to-door. I think one of your relatives even turned me away from him when it was evident that I might bash him over the head. Nevertheless, we chose a good place for you.*

*The spring greened the ground where we'd coffined and vaulted you safely from the elements. The small maple grew and I sat day after day, against the marble, talking to you. I had to tell you so much. So much had happened. So many things I wanted to hear your advice about. So many things you should have known, have witnessed. Like Clio's birth. I cried there. I cursed you there. I found peace there. I found forgiveness from you there. And in the silence of this place where your body was but a mere six feet from mine, I felt the safety of your embrace.*

# THE RAW ACHE

BED:

*The empty space*
*I crawl into at night.*

The body needs to be touched. It is as fundamental as food, air, warmth. Yet, when sucked into the whirlpool of grief, touch can burn instead of comfort. How strange that we retract so fast from the very touch that can heal us. Yet even a gentle touch can upset the delicate, fragile adhesive that holds together a person touched by death. An embrace could throw us into the treacherous caldron of memories—times when it was there and times when we only yearned for it to be there.

We clearly recognize that a badly burned person should not be touched. We can see the wounds as well as the pain. But in psychic pain we cannot see the parts of the person bleeding, raw. Perhaps someday scientists will be able to actually measure and see the complex and profound interweaving of attachments between people who love each other. Like cords, slowly threaded into the cells of two people, a tapestry of emotions as tangible as Siamese twins who share the same organs, the love binds them. When there is the death of one, what happens to the other? What happens to the tapestry that was woven over experiences that were shared, points of view that had merged, and emotions that had been grown, year after year? One day we will take the emotional pain of death as seriously as we take physical injury.

*There is nothing I yearn for now more than to be touched by you who can no longer touch me. The memory fades but the aching does not. I am human. I am alive. Perhaps needing touch proves how alive I still am. Sometimes my bed needs more than me in it. There must come a time when I allow someone into this sacred ground. It isn't possible that the person mean as much to me as the one I lost—I must begin the forgetting. I will try to allow someone to touch me so I can begin to heal.*

*I want the physical pleasure of a man's hair against the smooth skin of my hairless body, his hardness against my softness. I want to make him moan and ache for more of me, but I ache and moan for no one. It sounds hard of me. Maybe it is. I cannot say that the old belief about a widow's heart going to the grave with her dead husband is true. But neither can I say it is not true.*

*I learned to love many things about my late husband that I didn't like at first. I remind myself of this often when I contemplate dating. But as yet I am more content to be alone now. I say "more" content, for I have not reached contentment, but I remember now what it is. In my house is an echo* of the space a man would (could? can?) fill, but I cannot find a single inch of this home for sharing just yet. I long for human distraction in the evenings, but when someone provides it, I regret his intrusion. I would rather be making curtains.

At this point, I am no one's mate. No good to any man looking for a cork for his black hole or for a dance partner. My body aches to curl up next to someone I am safe with. But I am safe with no man yet, for I am not yet safe with me.

My muses tell me that this is a passing thing. Do I miss the familiarity of someone, or only the idea of it? Familiarity takes time, and time is something I am careful about investing in anyone. I haven't the patience or stamina to hang on long enough to find smelly feet endearing. I am still evolving into a new person, ever lonely, ever searching. I am far too selfish these days. Too self-centered. I feel no guilt about this. Yet, on the other hand, I need so very much that I hesitate to ask for anything at all. I am afraid that the very force of my needs will blast him (whoever him is) out of the room, out of my life, and there I will be, alone again.

For now, I listen to the roar of the silence within, a silence deafening enough to drown out the pretty words of any man who would have me.

# REALITY SHIFTS

CONCEPT:

*Something I do not grasp*

*without feeling it in the flesh.*

Memories fade. They are replaced with the new life we are living. Like a zoom lens, pulling back, the focal point changes. What was once so vivid, blurs. Try and hold on to yesterday and we become blind to today.

*When we picked the baby names, she was still a bulge in my belly. You were still alive. Your name was you. Jim. It spoke to me of a square jaw and high cheekbones. It was part of my name. Jim and Stephanie. But the baby's name was awkward. Clio, Clio. Lewis, Lewis. I said the names over and over, but there was no body attached to them. I knew only in theory that this baby was alive. But it had no sound, no scent. I could not hold it, or see toes wiggling through tiny booties. I could see your toes wiggling through socks with holes at the end because you never cut your toenails. I could smell you in the night,*

*that sweet smell that came from your chest. I could hear the rumbling timbre of your voice, a voice that seemed bigger than you. You were real. The baby was only a concept. What would this child look like? Would its voice be low like yours? The dreams of babies wafted through my life, still disembodied.*

*Then you died. Two weeks later, the baby moved inside me. You were still real, though. In my memory, I could hear your speech patterns. I could feel your legs against mine in sleep. I looked every time something moved out of the corners of my vision, believing I'd see you coming up the stairs. But you never came up the stairs again. You remained real to me, but slowly you were on your way to becoming a concept. Now the baby kicked me in the night, like you used to. It was inside me, but it wasn't a person to me yet. Your face began to fade from my memory. I knew, in theory, that the baby was real. I knew, in theory, that you were no longer real.*

*On the day she was born, I could not remember your face. You had made the full transition into a concept. All I saw now was her little face, her little lips suckling at my breast. She was twenty-one and a half inches long. She had a heart, bones, blood, and muscle, all in miniature. Miniature in flesh, but in spirit she monopolized my thoughts. Ah, she is hungry; ah, she is wet; ah, she is sleeping, snuggling, gurgling sounds. You became only a one-dimensional photograph, silent, stilled forever in a single pose.*

*But sometimes, when she smiles, I see your face open before me.*

# THE SAURIAN TAIL

EVIL:

*Systematic brutality,*

*usually done with an innocent expression,*

*which seeks to make insanity look sane.*

It is important to confront the topic of evil when dealing with grief because evil always causes grief. Certainly, not all grief comes from evil, but all evil produces loss. Big losses. The distinction between random cruelty—striking out in a time of distress—and evil are actually very simple. There is no conscience attached to evil. The shadow it casts over our values makes them seem trite. Evil parades as sanity so as to undermine our sense of reality. This is its biggest threat, for without reality we have nothing. We can lose our material possessions, our positions and titles, our jobs and careers, even our friends and families. But if we do not have a grip on basic right and wrong, and the boundaries around each of these, we are incapable of choosing. Loosely, this could be called insanity.

The topic of evil is controversial because of how closely it brushes up against fundamentalist religions. For many years,

I refused to believe that evil really existed. It was inconceivable to me that brutality could be done for no reason, or without guilt. That was, as I found out, because I am not evil. Most of us are not. But evil people do exist in our world. Seldom do they brandish horns. More often than not, they look perfectly fine. Even exceptionally good. They emerge at fortuitous times, usually when we are at our weakest, because evil will never seek an equal opponent. It is the hyena who waits until the prey falters before it moves in for the kill.

It is inevitable that evil will rear its head when death visits. In-laws never speak to us again after the funeral. No explanation. No reason. Just silent blame and the cruel desertion. Some of us have even had people say to us "I wish it were you who died." Death seems to stir the shadows of all involved and out of that caldron rise lies, deceit, and premeditated revenge of unprecedented brutality. Many of us who expected our families and friends to stand by us at our darkest hour found ourselves attacked instead. Not all of these attacks were evil. Some were reactions to the insanity of a person they loved being here one day, and gone the next. Like wounded animals, it is natural to attack when we are wounded. Or to look for someplace to put the blame, in order to make sense of the nonsensicalness of death.

Evil is different. Evil is calm. It looks sane. It acts systematically, with no regard for the carnage it leaves in its path. Evil people serve themselves and see other people purely as utensils for their own use. In extremes, they are serial murderers, cult leaders, terrorists, and pimps. They are easy to spot. But the evil people who populate our lives day-to-day are seldom so dramatic, seldom so brazen that they can be recognized. It is only when we are singed by their subtle but burning attacks that they become evident. If we are willing to call a spade a spade.

Evil is incapable of empathy. Evil people do not see us as people when they look at us, but instead see us as instruments for their ultimate ends. Since evil people do not feel what the vast majority of human beings feel, they haven't the capacity to empathize. Since their emotional bodies are vacuous, they have no regard for anyone else's emotions. Anything that gets in the way of their agenda should be eliminated. Evil people are entirely out of touch with their emotions. They don't feel sadness, remorse, guilt, shame, or pain. Perhaps they feel nothing at all.

Understanding the source of evil does nothing to excuse or amend the damage it does. I have seen and felt emotional atrocities that would have been violations of the Geneva Conventions had they been physical. Yet physical wounds heal far faster than emotional wounds. The intangible is hard to bandage.

No one wins or benefits from savage behavior. Nor can we reason with it, appeal to its humanity. This assumes evil is rational. Ultimately, we want to control it and stop it. But the chief intent of evil—to harm—is not a comprehensible intention to most people. It is, in an ironic way, right and healthy that we don't understand it. But as long as we fail to see evil for what it is, we are vulnerable to its power, fully engaged in keeping it alive and functioning.

These things are facts in death. The high drama, wills, and money often bring out the worst side of human behavior. Relationships are destroyed over a jackknife or a watch. People steal, lie, and cheat. Or they accuse others of doing the same. It happens. It is astounding how often it happens. But this is something we will confront in grief—betrayal that rubs salt into already bleeding wounds. People who don't experience this can count themselves lucky.

*It decimated my sense of reality. I found that everything I thought I could count on, I couldn't. People I thought cared for me, I discovered hated me. People I never knew cared for me came through as beacons of light.*

*My entire sense of what is what was challenged. I came to believe that I knew nothing anymore. I felt crazy. I felt as if I was losing my grip on reality. But the light side was that it made me a clean, blank slate, ready for the lessons and changes that would soon come.*

*Fighting evil by defending myself, or joining in on accusations and petty fighting, was simply playing into the hands of evil. It helped keep it alive and engaged. It offered opportunities to get down in the mud with it and fight it out. I made the decision that if I did that, I would be no better than those who were so cruel.*

*One of the hardest things I ever did was to not defend myself against things I knew were totally manufactured. I decided that I had to live a long time with the way I handled this situation, and I wanted to look at myself in the mirror and know that I maintained respect for myself and all others, no matter how they treated me.*

*This was the greatest lesson I've been blessed with, in understanding that I am responsible only for my behavior, not the behavior of others. I knew that if I played the game, I would only validate them. I searched inside myself, long and hard, for more hours than I cried over my husband's death, to see if what they said about me had any truth to it. I found it did not.*

*I decided not to give them anything of me, including my justifiable anger, because in the end they would have to look back at their behavior, as I would have to look at mine. I wanted nothing to be ashamed of. And I did not want to give them anything with which to blame me. I held my head up, and when it was unbearable, I screamed and yelled at them in the privacy of my therapist's office.*

*To this day, I am more proud of this than anything else I have ever accomplished. It took more stamina than I thought I had. It forced me to rely on good friends, and to discipline myself. After this experience, I know that I can do almost anything. Sometimes we have more to thank our enemies for than we have to thank our friends. As a dear Irish friend of mine says: "Ah, my enemies? God bless 'em—they make a better man of me."*

# So It Goes
# Like It Goes

MATURING:

*What happens if we're lucky.*

What an irony it is that as children, we impatiently await our next year. We want to be a grown up. We want to have all the benefits being a grown up seems to promise. Freedom, sweet freedom, from parental control. Then as we get older, we slowly begin to wish for younger years, lamenting wasted time, yearning for tighter skin, more hair, thinner thighs. We still are caught in the innocence of the idea that age keeps happening to us.

Until one day we realize that it stops. That when we die, we don't celebrate any more birthdays.

*You would have been fifty-five today. How lucky for the dead that they don't age. Aging pushed you forward with the high-pitch inevitability of a dentist's drill, and then it suddenly stopped, like the music in musical chairs, like a freeze frame at the end of a movie. Nothing more happens in life. Credits don't even roll over the last shot. You ceased.*

*I'll be thirty-seven this year. But I am just waking up, now nearly two years after your death. I want to go to the big time-keeper in the sky and ask for a couple of years' grace. After all, I was hardly awake these last two years, blocks of memory are gone, time compacted into a capsule that simultaneously whizzed by as it inched along.*

*"I can't be thirty-seven yet!"*

*I cry to the timekeeper, "I am just now getting off my knees." I was frozen for two years, and yet I grew more during that freeze than in all the previous seasons of my life combined.*

*The timekeeper smiles at me, mercilessly. There is no negotiating with him. He has the clock. "But I feel younger," I plead, "my spirit is more curious. My heart is more simple. My body is lithe and strong, like when I was twelve years old."*

*The timekeeper ignores my whining and continues moving the hands of the clock forward. I think I hear him say, "That is all good and well, my child, but you are growing older, nonetheless."*

*Age crawls along, dragging the youthful spirit through the mud of physical disintegration as the mind and spirit grow more and more wise. Now I think to be wise is to become more childlike. Now I step forward with the enthusiasm and curiosity that I see in my daughter. I dance more now. I sing more now. I laugh more now. I spend time, waste time, watching the grass grow and explaining the small and great things of life to Clio. But death marches forward, closer to me. And all I know is how much I don't know.*

*Thirty-seven is closer to forty than I'd like. Closer to no* more children, to a time I've designated since adolescence for the end of youth.

As my youth wanes, the glory of it transfers itself to my daughter. I can appreciate youth now more than when I was young. I watch her grow, massage her firm little back and legs, languish in her soft, taut skin, in her clear eyes, and in the rose color of her lips that will someday fade from years of lipstick and lip service to life's trivialities. I see her growing, discovering, playing, and I join her with the grateful perspective of having been there, once in innocence, and now in wisdom. I exalt in her smallest discoveries and lament the pain that will accompany her growing.

I'll be older if I'm lucky. You never will be.

# SOUL FULL

❧ ❧

SOUL:

*the energy that unites me with others*
*while paradoxically making me distinctly unique;*
*that which is left over for the living when someone dies.*

ometimes I tremble. I don't know what makes me tremble. I suspect it is a mixture of fear and excitement.
What I have experienced has changed me forever. Can I
tell you, really tell you, what it is like? You, reader, have you
trembled without knowing why?

My flesh is recyclable. I am simply atoms, magnetically
held together by this field of energy called a soul. I am matter. I am energy. I am chromosomes that give me a turned-
up nose and black hair. Do these manifest my soul? What
obligation do I have to these atoms that give me tangibility?
Do I owe other masses of atoms—my fellow beings—something also? I owe all beings, tangible, intangible, animate and
inanimate, honor and respect. As I brush up against them,
they validate my existence.

And how does this relate to us when we are ghosts?
Ghosts have given up the atoms that made them tangible to

others, so therefore—do they exist? Does energy exist without matter? Is the soul the energy that makes electrons orbit around the nucleus? And if that is true, then when these pieces of matter are disintegrated, is the soul released into the universe without any glue to keep it together? Does it stay together, or does it waft into all the other energy that swirls around the universe? Does it keep its own distinction, as those who believe in previous lives assume? Or does it blend into the tapestry of souls that have existed previously or will exist? Then, if it were to do this, who are we really? Are we all part of one another? Are we all part of the big One?

*Have I breathed in the energy that once held my dead husband's atoms together, so that energy now holds some of my atoms together? Is he part of me, after years of exchanging "living" molecules of saliva in kissing, breath in sleeping next to each other for years? He entered me and left me, and then there was our daughter, another energy field, gluing atoms together that are offsprings of our combined genes. His energy and mine bind her together so that she is a person. His energy, if it is his soul, and my energy, if it is my soul, united to form another soul. Separate. Distinct in herself. Yet resembling the eyes he wore, the nose I wear. In her, we joined as one. In her, we blended our souls through the conspiracy of energies.*

*So, is he really dead? As I look at her, as I walk through this life, doing things we would have done together, alone, I know that he is not here, but as I look at her, I also know that he is here. My natural, earthbound logic wants to tell me that something cannot be true and untrue at the same time. He is dead and gone, never to be seen, felt, heard again. Yes, I say to my earthly logic. Yes, this is true, as we know it.*

*But can I assume that there are other ways of knowing? Other ways of seeing that aren't bound to the limitations of cones and rods and retinas? Can I see through my heart? Can I see through that intangible soul that is one with all other souls on planes of existence where all things are known, where all time is moot, and where all limitations are simply a necessity for existence on a plane called earth?*

*When I hear a thought that is foreign to my normal way of thinking, is it Jim, giving me that thought, telling me what I need to know at that moment? When I have a dream, is it a time when I transcend my earthly form to join other souls for a night, so that they might teach me, cajole me, mystify me? When I have an awakening, an ah-hah!, is it my soul hearing what the other souls are telling me?*

# THEY LIE IN AMBUSH

ANNIVERSARIES:

*Days to stay in bed on;*

*times of remembering that throw us back emotionally,*

*into the past moments,*

*making our progress and lack of progress ever so clear.*

Oh, if only someone had prepared me for a setback on anniversaries. Anniversaries of births, deaths, special moments, dreadful times, triumphant victories can exhume past pain as if it were fresh. It seems to be an instinctual ritual performed by our subconscious that pays homage to the shadow of lost dreams.

Memories don't understand time. We expect to enjoy remembering or be unaffected by our memories. But anniversaries pluck at our subconscious, raising past feelings with no regard for the healing that has happened. It all seems for naught.

Even after years, we may anticipate that the anniversary of the death will no longer have an effect. Time has numbed the grieving, lulling us with the false security of normalcy.

Then we find ourselves in bed for the whole day, confused. But this is normal. We loved, and the imprint of that day rejuvenates both the love and the loss. Even if we convince our minds to forget, our cells remember. Expect this setback and be gentle to the part of the soul that doesn't understand the passage of time. It is only temporary. Anniversaries are days to contemplate the past, and glimpse the tremendous difference in this new life that survived.

*One year ago, you died. Today I look at grief. With a capital G. It's part of my life, as much as air, food, companionship, and love. Yet I fear it. Avoid it. Deny it.*

*All through my life I've given up things, people, places. I've given up illusions—about omnipotence, about immortality. I've given up friends who unexpectedly betrayed me. Friends who moved away. I found out I wasn't a whiz in science when I got a "C" on my fifth-grade exam. I found out that people lie, that parents break promises. I found out that my dreams of adolescence wouldn't be realized by my twenty-fifth birthday. I discovered that dreams go away, as do lovers, parents, and siblings, by death, abandonment, or a divergence of life's current. I discovered that the fantasy I had nurtured about someone loving me exactly the way I wanted was folly. I would never be loved that way.*

*I've given up many things in my life. And I have never been graceful about letting go. Either I thrust something away before it can leave me, or I cling like a pit bull on a postman's leg. When you died, I was not prepared for the deluges of feeling that would conflict with one another. I wasn't prepared to feel love and hate in the same moment. I was not prepared to push and pull at the same time. Perhaps that is why I am inert today.*

# Time to Divorce
# the Dead

SHEDDING LOYALTY:

*Allowing myself the self-confidence and love*
*I have needed so badly.*

Guilt is ever-present, waiting around each conquest to snatch our victory and dismiss it. It shows itself in what we think others think. Or that we even care. It appears as a phantom finger wagging at us as we move forward. When we shed our rings, when we kiss someone new. It casts a long shadow on the strides we make to recover, as if that was a betrayal of the dead.

This is not imagined. Often, the other people in our lives who haven't grieved as we have look to us to keep the dead alive by staying in our grief. If we move on to a new life, it means the dead are confirmed, really dead.

*The guilt of moving on seeps into my life every time I do something I thought I couldn't do without you. Every time I make a financial decision, I take over your job. Every time I fix the washing machine, choose a wallpaper without consulting you, I feel guilty. I rise to a new level of competence in each of these acts, yet I am anchored by the ballast of guilt. How dare I function without you! What could you have possibly meant to me if I can function without you? Much less, function well. I find that I have very good taste in decor, that I am a whiz at stock investments, that I can act as the general contractor on the renovation for my new house. How dare I?*

*Every so often I'm overwhelmed with the decisions. In those moments I hate you for leaving me. But I am stronger now, and I like being strong. I feel comfortable with myself for the first time in my life. And for this, I feel guilty.*

*And then there was the first time I kissed a man after you died. I felt that I was having an affair, not starting a new relationship. We were never divorced.*

*When can I stop proving that I loved you? When will I stop believing that loving you better might have saved you?*

*Would you please leave me to my new life?*

# A VISION QUEST

MAGIC:

*Something that still exists*

*if I listen*

*and follow the signs.*

*Something that breathes hope into me*

*when I least expect it.*

Magic exists all around us. Sometimes it is subtle—sometimes it is blatant. It pixilates through our lives, with no regard for whether or not we believe in it. But it is there, as surely as the air we breathe is there, though we can't see it.

It takes an acceptance of hope and life to see the signs magic places before us. Playful, sometimes even a little naughty, magic tugs at us, like a mute child who wants to show us something. Often we call it "coincidence," but there are no coincidences. What we would like to believe to be coincidence is really divine intervention. Don't try to understand—just follow the Yellow Brick Road.

*I really didn't know why I decided to go to Newport. All the original plans had fallen through, and no one was going to be there now. But I felt pulled and so I packed up the baby and babysitter, and went.*

*Within two days, I discovered what had compelled me to go. It happened on a windy day, when we didn't have anything to do. We just got in the car and drove. Every decision about which turn to take was done in the moment, and somehow, we ended up at the end of Cape Cod, in an art gallery.*

*There in the back was an exhibition of my friend Moti. I turned to the gallery owner and said, "I know Moti." She corrected me. "You knew him. He died three months ago."*

*A flood of memories came to me. He had been so important to me, like a kind old mentor. A decade of years had dulled his influence, the way he used to talk to me about writing as he painted. At an early age, he'd shown me the worker-bee part of art. Stroke by stroke, he worked. He took the mystery out of it so that I felt I could do it. He didn't speak to me about grand themes, but he embodied them.*

*Moti's paintings hung, each one speaking to me the way he used to. It was time for me to start working again. Word by word. Page by page. I could hear his voice. I could see his old and stubby body jumping around with the enthusiasm of a kid.*

*So far from home, every turn, an accident. I didn't have any reason to go to Newport. And I had not planned on going to Cape Cod. And of all the towns in Cape Cod, I drove into this one. And of all the galleries in that town, I walked into this one. And of all the artists that could have been exhibited,* it was Moti. A dear and genuine mentor. One of the few people in the world who could have gotten me to write again.

How was it that I got there? I didn't seem to be seeking anything. But standing there in the whirlwind of memories and conversations that once inspired me, I discovered how much it hurt to not be writing.

Maybe there is such a thing as magic.

# You Can Go Now

⚜ ⚜

GOOD-BYE:

*A word I can finally say, willingly.*

Time alone does not heal. It is the loyalty to life that heals. Loyalty to the inner *vis vitae* mends the scissions on our souls. Time and distance can give perspective, but time itself must not be mistaken for a healer, as so many platitudes would tell us. Feelings do not understand time, and what hurt us twenty years ago can be just as painful when another pain of the same sort strikes again.

There will be no perfect time when all of the threads are cut and tied off so neatly that saying good-bye will be entirely painless.

But somehow, in a place deep within the heart, there will be a moment when all that we held on to, out of our own longing, guilt, remorse, fear, will cease to be valuable. It will not be a happy time. But it will feel complete.

Time will not give this moment to us—only our willingness to be alive again.

Then we will be able to finally say, with heartfelt sincerity, good-bye.

*I held on to you after you died. Tight. For dear life. In the blackest of nights, I screamed into the hole you left—"You can't leave me! Not yet!"*

*Slowly, the healing loosened my grip.*

*Now I can feel you sometimes, still checking on me. I can feel you wanting to make sure that I'm okay. I can even see your face in the ethers when I close my eyes. I see it daily in our daughter.*

*I'm ready to let you go. Now that I've turned the drift of this boat around, now that I've found a new course, and a fresh wind to ride, I'm ready. You can go now. It was all those years together; they helped heal me. It was all those mountains we climbed—they came back to remind me of my mettle. It was all the love that we shared, and the living proof I have daily. These were my buoy in the storm.*

*Today I have given myself over to a new life. Oh, the guilt was crippling at first. I wanted to erase you entirely. But I have learned that nothing is pure, although some things can be almost pure. Now I have given the fathering of our daughter to a new man with only the faintest guilt. And to this new man I have given all my devotion, my love, my promises, and daily fulfillment of those promises. For this, I feel no guilt at all.*

*You sometimes come to me in my dreams now, a friend of a life once lived, a rhumb line on my life's chart, and a constant reminder that whether we like it or not, love can be a passing thing.*

*A life so fragile, a love so pure,*
*We cannot hold on but we try.*

*We watch how quickly it disappears*
*And we'll never know why.*
*But I'm okay now.*
*Goodbye my friend,*
*You can go now,*
*Goodbye my friend.*

—KARLA BONOFF, "Goodbye My Friend"